Journey to my First Step

A car crash survivor's story

Candice Puleo

DEDICATION

For John -

For better or worse, in sickness or in health. You have proved time and time again they are more than just words.

I am, as always,

Loving you

ACKNOWLEDGMENTS

I will never be able to adequately acknowledge those who were part of my journey. When people comment on what I have been through and how far I have come, I let them know it was because I was never alone, not even during the dark times when I thought I was. As you read this book you will see the importance of each of them.

So, a special thank you to the EMT who hugged me, the stranger in the ER who held my hand, the helicopter team that got me to where I needed to be, and the doctors (scores of them) that put me back together. Thanks to the aides that tried their best in hellish situations, the therapists that literally taught me how to live my best life however I could and got me back on my feet – both of them albeit not the way it was.

Thank you to my SCA Sisters whose prayers and continued contact reminded me God did not leave me but was in the car and is with me still.

Thank you to my dearest friends who got me through rehab and beyond, always surrounding me with love and brought normal at a time I desperately needed it.

Lastly to my family – thank you will never be enough. Their souls were as crushed by my situation as my body was, but they were my strength. No one should have to do for another what they did for me.

I am only here because of all of you.

I was a victim in a motor vehicle crash. My injuries are severe. I am navigating rehab where I am easily the youngest resident. There is no one who can help me understand this journey.

I turned to the internet. Cancer, alcoholism, drugs, death, and other losses. Nothing that fits my needs.

Then I remembered a blog by the country singer Rory Feek. He chronicled his life and his wife's cancer. He was honest and open. I remember how I felt following his story. So, I am sharing my journey. My middle of the night thoughts, my crazy, my support system.

I will reference a number of people directly. That by any means does not discount those whom I do not name. I will be honest; I will be open.

I will eventually take that first step.

B DAY -4

Attending a birthday celebration of my LLBFF in New York (Life Long Best Friend Forever). Wonderful day, good friends, great memories.

B DAY -2

As I don't "come home" often, we go to the cemetery as there is no one left to visit my family. Afterwards we have a fantastic authentic Italian lunch, and later pastries with the in-laws. Another good day.

B DAY (B IS FOR BOOM)

On the way to the airport to go back home to Florida, we are ~15 minutes into our drive when all 3 of us (LLBFF, her Significant Other [SO], and me) see something simultaneously. It's a blink, just like you see in the movies. I had no idea what it was I saw, or what was about to happen. There is no time to brace, no time to think. I hate to say, "the accident". This was just a blatant disregard for safety and general rules of the road.

So, I will say the BOOM was inevitable. My last recollection was realizing we all knew something was going to happen at the same time, then being thrown in the car. I was knocked out but woke up in the back seat not being able to see what was happening or what was going on. I felt for my cell phone and called my husband to let him know I was ok, but we were in an accident and to tell our son not to pick me up from the airport. I had no idea what the truth was, but I did not want anyone to worry. My next memory was being outside the car in tremendous pain. LLBFF was still in the passenger seat, SO was trying to assist me. I can't tell you how I got out of the car.

Time is going unbelievably slowly as we wait for the ambulance. The pain is unlike anything I ever felt at the time. Just when I thought I reached a pinnacle, it got worse. This loop continued on. LLBFF and I are transported to the hospital together. There is nothing to be done for the pain as my BP was dropping - so the ride to the hospital is torturous. The EMT starts to cut off my clothes. I understood my jeans as obviously something horrible had happened to my right side. But then went my Yankee socks and Derek Jeter Commemorative T-Shirt. I know we stopped so the EMTs could switch who was working on me. I also know I had passed out at some point from the pain. There are multiple times during this experience where I am awoken by loud noises which turn out to be me screaming. When someone asks you on a scale of 1-10 your pain level, all I can say is there is no number high enough.

I am not expecting a good outcome and my thoughts are that I love my husband and kids and wanted them to know that. If anything had happened my last thoughts were of them.

When we get to the hospital I am taken for a scan. I felt like I was a porcelain plate that was smashed to smithereens, every movement shattering me more and more. I wake to see SO; my LLBFF was in another ER room as she hurt her leg and we could not be together, but her concern was I shouldn't be alone. See why she is my LLBFF? When I wake up again one of LLBFF's friends is holding my hand. I can't speak and am in and out of consciousness, but this stranger spoke to me softly. The woman holding my hand, whom I only met once, is what defines the phrase "the kindness of strangers". I am truly thankful, more than I can ever express.

I awake again surrounded by hospital personnel and my friends. The hospital could not treat the extent of my injuries. WTF!? Where do they send you when a hospital states, "you are too injured"? This is worse than I could have imagined. My mind races as I have moments of clarity even though I still cannot speak. My *brain works* but I can't convey that to anyone.

I am told I will be sent by helicopter to a Level 1 Trauma Center. However, John is my next of kin and I must consent for them to let the people who are in the same physical state I am in to know where they are sending me. I believe he was on the phone as I tried my best to give consent. Shit gets real very fast. I see the helicopter crew and then am given what I will for forever describe as helicopter drugs. I am seeing in cartoons. The EMT comes in to hug me, looking into my eyes as she states, "You will be ok". When I open my eyes, I am in the helicopter but close them again because the cartoons are awesome. Best part of the day. Sadly, I have no real recollection of the ride itself – bummer. However, I will unequivocally say that is a ride I never want again.

At days end I remember pain, seeing my husband John, and then realizing I am in traction with rods through my leg. I have no idea it is hours and hours later and we are deep into night.

Aside - while medicine is science and I appreciate all the amazing things accomplished, medicine is just as much carpentry and plumbing. I would like to know who was doing helicopter drugs when they thought of "fixing" a person by drilling into a perfectly good leg bone and hanging a weight.

These are the highlights of memories that are my nightmares. They remain vivid, and I believe will continue for quite a while.

HUMPTY DUMPTY

My official diagnosis is I have an acetabulum fracture – feel free to Google it. Simply the socket that holds the ball of my hip went kablooey and as a result I had a dislocation (hence the traction) in addition to more pieces/parts than I had prior. I am not stable enough to have surgery straight away. I ask for a 2nd opinion who also concurred that I would not make it off the operating table alive until I was stable. I wait days for surgery, still not realizing how significant it will be. I cannot move. I question in my head if I will ever be able to again. When it is done, I am Humpty Dumpty in the flesh – put together with plates and screws.

Strike that. I am f'ing Ironman. What does not kill you makes you stronger. This bed will not define me.

ROOMMATE #1

Imagine being at the very worst place in your life-ever. Emotions running rampant, pain, anxiety through the roof, unable to move. Having to watch your loved ones watch over you. Now let me introduce you to bat shit crazy Beverly (BSCB). Based upon the volume and frequency of drugs BSCB asks for, as well as the fact she was administered Narcan in the hospital I was led to think she was detoxing. Nay Nay! In for something totally different. Add to that she is a hoarder. She is on the phone all day long to food services asking for things. All day long. Food, drinks, snacks, condiments. Which led to our "Late night guest".

BSCB is having a shit fest. She is screaming, pulling out her cell phone. Calling people outside the hospital to tell them about the giant roach in our room. Sending texts of the pictures to whom she is talking. To the **outside who cannot help.** Reminder – I am bed ridden.

Finally, the hospital staff is alerted to the un-paying resident. We are to change rooms. In the middle of the night. They will be working on eviction after we are moved. No one says the obvious – the hoarding situation led to the unwanted guest. BSCB packs and moves garbage to our new room. I sigh in my bed. Bonus is BSCB's phone does not work, and she is having withdrawals not being able to call to add to her stash. The hits just keep coming.

MY FAMILY, NOT ONE DROP OF SHARED BLOOD

After helicopter drugs your mind starts to go back to normal. Most frightening part? What will you see when you open your eyes? I see my family.

My husband and I have known each other since we were 15. I hate when people say "he/she is my life". He is not my life. *He is who I chose to build my life with.* There is a big difference between the two similar but vastly different statements. I would choose the latter every day and twice on Sunday. LLBFF of course. In laws.

Sappy feel-good moment: people come in and out of my room like going through a turnstile. Each one polite and introductions abound. I am hitting my button as much as I can for pain meds, and I am tired. I stop introducing people. John's dad introduces himself as my father. Again, and again and again. I think about this and cry. My dad died when I was 14. I have known this family since I'm 15. He is my father. They are my parents. The words in law will never come out of my mouth again.

Save for my children whom I would never want to see me in such a situation I have all the family I needed. My heart is broken into as many pieces as my bones when I see the reflection of them looking at me. I wonder more often than I will ever admit if that driver realizes how many lives he forever changed.

SO, WHAT IS AN ASS TABLET?

For the record nothing will ever compare to helicopter drugs. But being able to click a button every few minutes for IV morphine or dilaudid was ok. Our Primary Doctor calls John, who hands me the phone. *After* I hit the button. All I could tell him was my ass tablet was broke. I told him that's not right, but he knows what an ass tablet is. My father patiently says acetabulum over and over. For me I will have forever broke my ass tablet. I explained I pushed the button and hand John back the phone.

NEXT STEP IS NO STEPS AT ALL

There is no going directly home from the hospital. Travel is out of the question for quite a while. I cannot walk. I can put no weight on my leg for an estimated 8 weeks.

I cannot move. I cannot turn, I cannot get up. Don't listen to the song, everything is connected to the hipbone. They need to see if I can get out of the bed. It takes over 45 minutes with a nurse just to move to a sitting position, which exhausts me, so I lay back down with help, twenty minutes later than when we started.

I cannot care for myself. The level of care and rehabilitation needed requires me to be a resident in an acute rehab center. I ponder the irony that my ring tone is Amy Winehouse's Rehab. Great song – listen to it. John, my educated shopper, goes on the hunt for a rehab center that can support my level of injury. I can see his stress level has achieved nuclear. He finds scenic views, modern facilities - but there is no bed available when my time comes. The social worker is less than useless. Finally, we found a 5-star rated center for therapy. We decide therapy and the need to learn to walk outweighs a view. Days later off I go on another ambulance drive.

HOME SWEET HOME – NOT SO MUCH

We were told by the nice lady who gave me a teddy bear in the hospital that the rehab center was equipped for my injury. $20 bet anyone? Of course not, it would be a sucker bet. A condition of leaving the hospital is there is no more button pushing. The rehab center cannot administer narcotics until the Doctor signs off. He is late. The initial staff was not briefed on how to handle my injury. During the intake the pain has reached epic proportions.

I cry.

ROOMIE #2

The medium age of residents here is 30 years older than I am. Disclaimer; I am compassionate to other people's afflictions. Until my ass tablet broke. I am now Job from the Bible and am awaiting the locusts. Privacy curtain drawn I hear my neighbor speaking. I assume she is on the phone. Nay nay again. Instead of sleeping she believes she is elsewhere and needs someone to turn off the kitchen light. This goes on and on and she is ignored as of course everyone else but her knows there is no kitchen outside the door.

Until she screams to me (and for the nurses) that someone is breaking in through the air conditioner to kill us. Her Paul Revere routine goes on and on. She is then again ignored. Until the falling woman. Roomie to the rescue again calling the nurses to help the falling woman. They come in to assist, they think I am the woman she is calling about. Alas they were too late. The woman fell. On the tv. This is my night. In the morning I beg to be moved. A new room it is. I see a pattern here.

REHAB DAY 2

I had to be assessed. Every inch of my body was inspected under a microscope of strangers. Sad smiles are everywhere when I am asked to move. I cannot move my right side. Everything is connected to this ass tablet.

Smiles and praise are given when I wiggle my toes, like you would do with a small child who places a block correctly.

I cry. This too will be a pattern.

REHAB NIGHT 2

Only those closest to me know the horror of night 2. The educated me write emails at midnight to start someone on righting these wrongs. There is no help. I cannot move. I am at the mercy of strangers who know nothing of me.

I cry, again.

In the morning I gather people to make sure I will be taken care of. I am Ironman again. I have this. Until I see John and I break further. This was never my intention. He too goes to right the wrongs. He is my champion.

He will be leaving.

FINE DINING

The food at rehab is akin to a Michelin Star restaurant. This is where you will learn I am often driven by sarcasm. I am a picky eater (insert snickers here). This is less than edible. I must formulate a plan.

Breakfast is doable if you stay away from the "scrambled eggs". If you cry you can get pancakes. I get pancakes.

They have 2 selections for each meal, and things that are *always available* like hamburgers. I figure if I watch what I order I can get at least enough food to keep up my strength. I am also relying on gifts of food. They want you to eat in the day room. "It's not healthy to stay in your room" they say. If you eat in the day room, you get what you get. If you go downstairs, they have table service, and you can pick from the 2 selections or the always available menu.

I am not allowed downstairs without an escort. Who are they kidding? I can't get in a wheelchair with less than 2 people helping. John and I tell the desk we will be eating dinner downstairs. Our time is limited as he cannot stay the duration of my rehab. We want to pretend as best we can that things will be ok. When the time comes, he is my escort. We roll up to a lovely table for 2. Then wait.

Someone comes by to ask my name, like they are checking my reservation. We wait. Another person asks for my name. We wait. There is a woman with drinks. I ask for one and she simply states I have no glass. My response is I didn't know this was a bring your own type of glass of establishment. No one comes back.

I tell him if they ask for my name again, I will say it is Victoria Parker. That will be my witness protection name if ever needed. Victoria so I can keep part of me and Parker – like Peter Parker aka Spider-Man. It's a good name. I will never be Vickie or Tori; Victoria is how you can find me. Hmmm, now that everyone knows my plan, I may have to change that. You can see my mind is wandering. That happens a lot now. It's hard to concentrate and words are eluding me at times.

Finally, someone comes by with a tray of food. Wait!? What happened to my choice? I am to have a choice! With everything that I have lost so far, with the loss of control of my life, I cannot give up what little say I am allowed to have. They tell me I had to let them know I was coming. I told them I did – 3 hours before. Ironman has this. I will not eat this "vegetable lasagna" placed before me. They offer it to John. He is appalled. He would starve rather than subject himself to the mysterious items on that plate. Me? I ask for a burger. Off she goes. The drink lady states I still do not have a glass. Server comes back to state they have no burger. Apparently, whoever oversees procurement is falling down on the job with glasses and food. So much for the always available menu.

I ask what else do they have. A suggestion of a meatball hero is made. Sold. When the dish is brought out, they also find a glass. I ask for apple juice in my stemware glass. The finest Mott's 2018 reserve they have. They do not appreciate my humor. Sarcasm is lost in this place. The hero is 3 Ikea like meatballs on a hotdog bun. I can get through 2.

WHEN YOU'RE GONE

John will be leaving. He cannot stay and sit with me for 2 months. I will break if he does. The swelling is so bad from the trauma I cannot wear my wedding ring. My armor has a kink.

WHY I AM HERE – MY REHAB JOURNEY

I was in a hospital bed unable to move. The bed would not define me. I was able to move to a chair with much assistance. It took 45+ minutes the first time I tried to sit up with help and I'm not improving on that much. I've got nothing but time. This will not define me.

I am brought down to rehab and am assessed. I am in a giant wheelchair to keep my injuries safe. I tell them I will work harder than anyone and to push me. I have a goal; to get back home. They agree after my assessment to have both occupational and physical therapy 6 days a week. At this time, I believe this wheelchair will be a large part of my life for a long time coming.

In my mind I am Mario Andretti, and the wheelchair is my race car. In reality I am winded just getting in. As I try to practice, I crash into everything. John keeps jumping in to help. He keeps asking me what I am doing. I told him I must practice. To learn. In my head I add "to learn to live like this".

We both realize maneuvering a wheelchair is like parallel parking. Not my strong suit. Rehab is old so I can only hope they don't notice all the scrapes and dings. We switch my wheelchair to one I can use a bit better.

Again, my motivation is to get back together with my family. Other motivation? Answer these for me.

    1.   What do you do if your foot itches?

2. What do you do if you are cold?

3. What do you do if you need a drink?

4. What do you do if you drop the tv remote?

5. What do you do when you have "to go"?

All my answers are to call for help. And wait until someone can come. I will regain independence. Ironman.

ON MY OWN – JUST FOR A MOMENT

John leaves today. I am breaking again inside but trying to be Ironman. Until it is time for him to go. I do not have my wedding ring. As we hug and kiss goodbye, I will have no tangible piece of him with me for the first time in 28 years. But he remains in my heart.

I have not showered since the Boom I have not washed my hair. I feel alone and broken and am at my absolute worst. I put on my Yankee cap. And then my LLBFF & SO arrived. They can take me outside to the garden. We sit, we laugh, and for a moment I forget. Our most photogenic friend appears. She says nothing about my appearance. She brought goodies to eat. This is my family, they are happy to see me, truly happy. I've got this. This chair does not define me.

LOVE AND MISS... COFFEE

Rehab is still a hospital setting. Poking, prodding, blood draws, medicine, doctors, and nurses asking questions and examining you. All day long. Starting at 5 am. Reminder most rehab patients are geriatric. Food is bland,

soft, and coffee is watery and decaf. They use a food service that caters to the 99.99% of the residents. I can't remember when I last had a good cup of coffee.

My Occupational Therapist (OT) asks me during a session if I want coffee. Still have not showered, I am sweaty, out of breath, pushing myself to limits I didn't know I could surpass. He mocks me with coffee. I look him the eye and say this decaf shit is no coffee and haven't I suffered enough? He looks back at me and says 4 words that warm my heart - "I have a Keurig".

I savored that cup like a fine wine. He states I now know your motivation. If I ever want coffee, I have to get the 30 feet to the coffee maker and do it myself. Up to this point I have only walked around 15 feet.

It is important I define "walking". Use of a walker, holding on for dear life as I shuffle using only one leg, someone holding on to my shorts/arm. Always getting a wedgie. Another person pushing my wheelchair behind us. If I could take a video, I think there is a possibility of a $10k prize.

The next day, I made my way the 30 feet. I can't tell you how long it took. However, the other residents stopped what they were doing and cheered me on from the sidelines. They were with me as I dragged myself across the room dripping in perspiration. In victory I slap the counter and turn to the OT. He tells me, "Make it yourself. I am not your husband". This is one of his important lessons, his tough love. I have to learn to live, like this. His job is to teach me, to prepare me for real life. He must assume that each day I work with him may be as much as I recover, His mission is to teach me to live in my new world.

TEARS OF JOY

The therapists are pushing me. I tell them push harder. They are MacGyver, trying to figure out the best way for me to heal, to gain strength, to use tools to gain independence. More. I still want more.

So, I am again "walking". I go 50 feet before I can go no more. I am getting kudos and thumbs up from the other residents. They get me down on a therapy table and – guess what – I cry.

The Physical Therapist (PT) thinks I am hurt. I tell her these are happy tears. That a week ago I did not see myself ever getting out of that chair. I told her I know now I will walk, eventually, with pain and a limp, but I will walk. We hug. She pushes me harder. I am going to be ok.

QUESTIONING MY FAITH

I am angry. I am angry at the driver; I am angry at the world. I am most angry with God. If this was the only tragedy I would have experienced, my take on the BOOM may have been different.

Not long ago I was volunteering at a charity with my team from work. One of my jobs was to wash pots and pans in the kitchen for those preparing food for the less fortunate. I volunteered for this thankless assignment. It was hot and wet. I worked harder than I do at my own home. This is only example. But one that is rolling around in my head at night when I cannot sleep or move.

Knock, knock God. How about balancing the scales? Is this how good deeds are repaid?

I was raised Catholic. Went to Catholic school through and including college. My mother worked in our rectory. Nuns would come for dinner just like they were my aunts. I taught catechism and was a lector at my church. John and I got married in my parish by the Monsignor who did not even let us kiss in church.

Yet I struggle with the current institution that is the Catholic Church. It has been difficult taking the stories of my youth of forgiveness, compassion, and doing what is right to what has become the business side of the Church. I won't go into all the "laws" that I cannot follow in good conscience that are opposite of how I know Jesus. Faith, to me, became more than following the rules of a bunch of men in Rome and is more aligned with being a good person. I am not perfect. I fail, I slip, I do things that I know better. But in my heart God grants me forgiveness. So how do I make it through this struggle especially knowing what is before me?

I reached out to a very special group of women I went to high school with, many whom I have not seen since graduation. Through the power of social media, we have been connected again for some time. We are better as women than we were young girls. These are strong women, and women of faith. I tell them my situation and ask for prayers to give me strength.

I cannot do justice to the outpouring of love and prayers I have received. Offers to come see me, bring me anything I need, to call any time day or night. They understand if I do not respond. They are helping me understand that God never left me, nor does he plan to do. God is not Superman who sweeps down to save the damsel in distress. He is the parent who watches over his children. He was in the car. He is suffering as I suffer. He will be my strength.

Behold thy strength and thy glory:
Woman. Pure. Enlightened. Tender and wise. My SCA sisters

THE YANKEES AND MY GERIATRIC CREW

So being in NY the Yankees are the team. One day in my Yankee hat I wheeled into the day room for a meal. I figured I should try it at least once.

I am across from an elderly gentleman who is most likely in his 90s. He looks at my hat and asked how the Yankees did. I smile and tell him they won. We make our introductions. He then asks me, "do we like the Yankees?". I tell him with gusto we love the Yankees. He hits his companion and repeats we love the Yankees. At times he has amazing moments of clarity and can remember things way in the past. Other times we bond that we love the Yankees.

The wildcard game is the hot conversation at therapy. Ladies I have never heard utter a sound before are questioning the lineup. We rally around our team. Turns out the game is on a TV station we do not get. I use my tablet and the Direct TV app and watch the game in my bed. They win and it's a good day.

Craziness ensues the next morning as I talk about the game with my therapist. The residents ask how I saw it if it was blacked out. Trying to explain technology in basic terms, they too now "need the app".

I tell them if the Yankee/Red Sox game is blacked out and we get permission I will bring my tablet in the day room so we can listen to the game together. I am slowing building my crew

WALKING DEAD

I like zombies. I have a nice collection of t-shirts that depict various characters and/or sayings. My shirt today has mixed reviews at rehab. It says "Kill all Walkers". Others do not find it as funny as I do as I wear it as I zombie shuffle around rehab amid the wheelchairs.

BOOM POST OP – MEETING MY SURGEON

When you are in the hospital doctors buzz around you like flies. After you leave the hospital, you need to come to them. My first field trip. Apparently, I have people now who handle these things. I am told they have "secured transport". Am I going in an alien spaceship? Nope. Converted van/ambulette for which my insurance states is not needed. Can't the doctor come to me? With his staff? And x-ray tables? I will not go into issues with insurance now because I am pretty sure there will be a lot more to discuss later.

My people tell me I need an escort. Why? Do you think I'm not coming back? Pops to the rescue.

So how does one get magically moved from rehab to a medical building? My last few transports varied so. I stay in my wheelchair and the back of the van opens. Some modified tailgate lift comes down and I am pushed on.

Please read the following in your best Roseanne Rosandana voice without pausing…

You know that feeling when you are on a roller coaster, and it is chugging up up up and you are starting to get a little sick to your stomach and you hope you don't pass out or throw up? Yup, that's me.

I am told I do not need to hold onto the handles. I can only think "this is how I die". I survived 2 car accidents and am going to go splat backwards, and nothing is going be able to stop me. The driver grabs the handles and jumps on the lift behind my chair. I think he must have been a carnie ride operator in his previous profession.

I am overjoyed at how solid the lift looks (again if you do not know me well, that was written sarcastically). Once pushed, the chair is secured like cargo on a tractor trailer. I look up. Should there be another crash the chair will be safe, but I will be though the windshield. I feel like I am living in a Final Destination movie. He eventually comes back and straps me to the chair. Thank God for small miracles.

Off to the doctor. X-rays needed of course. The tech was incredibly gentle. I would like her as a friend. I stop short of asking if she has a Facebook account and will friend me. Nonetheless I am achy. Pops wheels me back and forth from place to place like I am fragile and would break. If I oversaw my wheelchair, I would have taken out 10 people and left a path of destruction.

In the room waiting on the doctor, the x-rays are put on a large screen. My heart stops. And yes, I cry. This is the first I see of how broken I was/am. I researched broken ass tablets and there are 10 patterns of breakage. I look at my x-rays and now think there must be 11. I ask Pops for a tissue (*** pause*** I am typing Pops because I keep trying out names for my new mom and dad). I dab my eyes, shake it off. Ironman is in the house.

The doctor comes in. He is not who I remember. I ask did he assist? He told me he operated. Hmmm, will need to find out more info later. My mind is still fuzzy on a lot of things. I point to the x-rays and ask him to walk me though what we are looking at. He does, very succinctly. We discuss the damage, how it looks now, treatment plans, going home, going to work, Driving (all things now in my future, distant, but still). I leave feeling better, ok truthfully nauseous from the day, but emotionally better. Which makes no sense. I got no concrete answers. But I left with a host of possibilities.

TODAY'S INSTALLMENT IS BROUGHT TO YOU BY THE LETTER S – FOR SUPER

SUNDAY SHOWER!!!!

I have not showered since before the BOOM 19 days ago. Please ponder that for a moment. I was able to have my hair shampooed once by the "beautician". It was an ordeal I will talk about at another time.

My 30 staples were removed which now cleared me for a shower. Sunday is our "free day"- no OT no PT. Well, that's for everyone else. I have weekend homework from my therapists. Push push push.

I will admit they kind of forgot about me last night as I am at the end of the hall. The aide came in to get me ready for the night, but hey, the Yankees were on. I told her I am staying up to watch the game on my tablet. She didn't come back, and I never pushed the call button. Side note: I feel badly for my crew. They cannot stay up and out past their allotted time schedule. So, no game in the day room. I tried.

I fell asleep in yesterday's play clothes. When the morning aide saw that, she was concerned (heartwarming moment here) that I was not taken care of. Told her I was up watching the game and wanted to be left alone to have one night of normal. She smiled. Then I went in for the kill – let's talk shower.

She said we could get one in quick before breakfast. Nope. I am not having that. I want to revel in the luxurious feeling of hot water cascading as I shampoo and condition with my own products. I kindly stated I knew she would be hectic with breakfast so just come see me when she has some time.

When she comes back, I feel a bit like BSCB – we have packed clothes, towels, washcloths, my scrubbing tool, shampoo, conditioner. I look like a pack mule. I don't care.

Into the shower room. There are multiple "stalls" so several residents can shower at the same time (single sex only). I have a concern as the chair (a contraption made from PVC pipe) is lower than what I am used to. We forge on. She helps me strip in my wheelchair which is not an easy feat and helps to transfer me to the shower PVC shower throne. Shower was the best thing ever. I feel clean. I feel human. I feel like I am getting my life back.

Someone knocks on the door. A gentleman resident wants to shower. I look my aide in the eye and state I have not showered in 19 days. He will have to wait as I am not rushing through this. She tells him and his aide, shower room is occupied, and he will just have to wait until we are done. I think Ironman found a side kick.

For those who have never been under prolonged anesthesia, it kills your hair. Dries it out, makes it brittle. Being able to condition my hair is bonus level 1000+.

If I thought my first try of getting up in bed was time consuming, try getting dried and dressed after a shower while in a wheelchair. They don't cover that in OT. By the time you are done you need another shower.

I also had a productive morning. I "cleaned" my room. Which truly just amounts to figuring out where to put things so I can get them and making sure my dirty clothes are put in the laundry bag. I also move my garbage can. Someone put it behind where my wheelchair goes. Might as well be on the moon. I practice putting on a sock and shoe (45 minutes seems to be my magic time, that's how long it took me to put on one sock the first time by myself). I am using all the tools I have been given and told to practice with. I cannot do anything by myself without them. I am understanding the term handi-capable. I got my own clothes rather than someone just pulling something out of the draw. These tasks took the entire morning.

SUCCESS

I need a nap.

Those 4 words are very significant to me. I have been fighting and pushing and working and doing everything and more my therapists are asking of me. I used my adaptive tools to get ready this morning. I did my OT, am I going to make it to the end?

Eventually my tired body won the fight and I call the aide to help me get in bed. She is surprised. They are all watching my progress, my fight. She looked at me like I was the expected winner of a match that took a hit and is going through a 10 count. All I could say is I'm tired. I need a nap.

I put the tv on and the movie The Fault in Our Stars was playing. I have seen this god awfully depressing film before. Think Ole Yeller sorrowful but with teens with cancer. Yet I didn't change the channel. Why am I putting myself through this? Don't I have enough to be sad about? I can't say for sure.

I can only think that I am in GO GO GO mode. The thought of stopping is akin to failure which is not an option. Never did I think this pattern was not sustainable. Yet my body, this temporarily broken vessel, is a machine. The machine needed maintenance. I am not bottling up my feelings. I am coping. Yet sometimes there is no time for me to just feel. I have a goal to be achieved, I can have my pity party at another time.

But laying in this bed, a soft, warm blanket wrapped around me, watching that movie brings me comfort. If I were home, I would have snoozed on the couch with a sad chick flick playing in the background. This need to take a break does not diminish my work here but was a reminder of what normal is. Sometimes you get tired, you need to take a break, to relax and watch tv while you nap. I seemed to have forgotten that.

I make sure I am up 1/2 hour before PT. Out of bed, in the chair, ready to go. I had more range of motion today than previously and I drag my sorry broken ass tablet almost 150 feet with a few stops in between. #powernap

I DROPPED MY BLANKET

Rehab is my home for the foreseeable (time yet to be determined) future. But it's not my home. If home is where the heart is, my home was definitely back in Florida, 1250 miles away. Yet it also will take a lot of heart to get me back to where I need to be physically (broken body and geographical).

I am in essence in a hospital room. LLBFF tried to cheer it up with decorations however I was not feeling it. You can put lipstick on a pig but it's still just a pig.

But today most favored aid (MFA) who makes sure I am **showered**, made my hospital bed with my Yankee blanket, a gift from SO.

I have been using it as a throw blanket, or just on the side of my bed and use it when I need a little cuddle as it is super soft. She looks at me and says, "just a little somethin' somethin'".

So, I go to bed and watch my beloved Yankees blow what should have been theirs to take. It's like they didn't even care to try the last 2 games. They worked so hard all season and then just stopped. I would be lying if I tell you I had a sidebar with God telling him a win would go a long way to make up for my unfortunate circumstances. I guess he was busy elsewhere.

I turn off the game and try to sleep. I finally manage a few hours then need to use the restroom.

Click the button. Reposition the bed. Start to use adaptive tools to move this useless leg. Another sidebar: while I say useless, PT is working. I am able to move slightly which is better than zero. OT has also trained me on how to get it moved using what is referred to as a pony strap. It is a long strap with a handle on one end and a loop on the other. You try to hook your foot so you can gingerly drag your leg in the direction you need it moved inch by inch. Only one of a bag of tools at the ready. There is an adaptive tool for every task you have to undertake, and I need them all. They stay by my side on my bed as there is nothing I can do without assistance. I have to use bed rails once the leg is moved to try and position myself to get ready to sit up.

Then I wait. And wait. The time is not horrendous but when you are like, "I have to pee" you must concentrate to let your body remember this is not a 2-minute thing for you to get to the toilet.

The nurse comes in; the night aide must be assisting another resident. At night there is 1 nurse, and 2 aides for ~40 people. She positions the wheelchair and helps me the remaining steps to sit up. I then position the walker, stand from the bed with a crutch, use the walker to get in the wheelchair and roll to the toilet. Similar steps to use the bathroom. Then reverse it all to get back to bed. I can't wait for the 2-minute pee again.

When I am settled, and she leaves I see my blanket is on the floor. I got this. I reposition my bed, grab my adaptive tools I use to help get dressed, and it takes 10 minutes, but the blanket is on the bed. I am sweating, I am tired. I am thirsty. I have decided to skip taking a big drink of water as that will quicken the need to do this all over again.

I could have taken my disappointment at my team who let me down and left that blanket on the floor for someone else to get later (PS: they wash the floor every day, so I am ok with the fact it fell). Or I could understand shit happens, you don't always get the outcome you hoped for, and you pick up and start again. It was after 4 in the morning at that point. I would be lucky if I got back to sleep, but I chose not to leave the blanket on the floor. I chose to pick up and keep going. #metaphorforlife

LITTLE FEEL-GOOD MOMENTS BROUGHT TO YOU BY REHAB

Dance parties rock.

One of the residents was being discharged. They have a tradition at rehab that at your last therapy session you have a dance party. A Latin music station is put on – Shakira is in the house. This semi-elderly woman holds onto her walker and starts twerking and shimmying. My hip hurts just watching. This goes on for several minutes. Hands up in the air as this was a true celebration. My therapists turn to me and say get ready, that will be you soon. I hate to tell them I am missing the dance gene. I guess I can YouTube some moves. I have a few months left. Residents making strides

This seems to be a good week for several residents. They graduated to canes or were getting ready to be discharged within the week. Equipment is "signed out" to residents as needed. For the most part standard nondescript wheelchairs and walkers. But oh, the canes! Colors and sparkles! Not my style but I am also younger than 80.

It's like Harry Potter with the wands and the sorting hat. Which cane works for which resident? Once the correct one is chosen, we all clap. A cane is one step away from home.

FRIENDS

I am still not good company. I truly feel bad turning down offers for visits. I will get there, just not yet. However, I have an exception for two ladies that have been part of my life for so long and have been with me at my worst and best. I am comfortable talking about nothing, the BOOM, rehab, and ways to get the remaining glue off my body. People say they should make airplanes out of whatever the black box material is. Screw that. Use the glue from tape in the hospital. I believe that I will still have glue on me when I retire.

So, we sat tonight, shared burgers and fries and laughed. Normal. My life can be normal.

SURPRISE

The 'rents came by for a visit and to give me clean clothes. Nice visit as always (I only cried 1x). When it was time for them to leave, I had a surprise. I held onto the arms of my wheelchair and stood on one leg (think flamingo like) to hug and kiss them goodbye. I am gaining strength, and this was a milestone. Happy tears all around. Hugs and kisses for everyone.

STUFF

All of the residents have equipment, most of it the same. They label everything here with your initials and bed number. Should you drop/leave something it can easily be returned to your room.

I get that. But really, is it necessary for me to have a bracelet on with the same identifier? Do they lose people often? I assert my independence and cut it off.

VISUAL AID

I thought at this point I would not have to explain my injuries anymore. Who am I kidding, I will be explaining this the rest of my life. LLBFF to the rescue, as a visual aid, she gives me a toy skeleton. I color with a silver marker all the places I have titanium pieces. I may need a second marker.

GUESS WHAT?

Ironman has been working on the armor. Swelling in my hand is down enough to put my wedding ring back on. Little victories need celebrations.

Potassium one of the seven essential macro-minerals

I've said before rehab is a hospital setting, which includes the constant monitoring, blood pressure, finger sticks, temperature taking, meds throughout the day and occasional blood Draw. Most times I get "all good Candice" (they are not my friends, so they don't call me Candi), "very good Mrs. P.", "go eat/drink something your levels are low."

Until yesterday. I am fatigued. I feel exhausted. My muscles are sore. I attribute these feelings to my healing body pushed by daily therapy. Every day I do more, go further. I yearn for just one night to sleep in my own bed on my side or belly. In my mind that is all I need to re-energize.

On the way back from pt (they now just drop me off at the nurses' station and I am to wheel myself back to my room to strengthen my muscles, plus I have all the time in the world as I am not going anywhere) the nurse stops me in the hall. My blood work came back with high levels of potassium.

Ok. So what?

She says they have a stat order to treat me. STAT? That's new.

They ask about symptoms – fatigue, muscle ache, etc. I tell them yes but how can I tell the difference between working at therapy and something else? I can't, they can't either. They give me 2 shot glasses full of what I will describe as liquid chalk. Apparently when there is muscle trauma this is something that could occur. If untreated it could affect my heart and kidneys. I won't bitch about them waking me up again to check my vitals and take blood. Good catch rehab medical.

INSPIRATIONS FOR MY STORY

Sometimes the enormity of a small task overtakes me. Other times I can't help but see some semblance of humor in dealing with my current situation or yet other times it's a text or a conversation that sparks inspiration.

To sound like a broken record, I am in a hospital room. With a hospital bed, wheelchair, a walker, crutches, an abduction pillow, and a host of adaptive tools. There is barely room for me. They have accommodated me by giving me the window bed. This serves two-fold, I have a view to an outside world that I cannot currently partake in, and it gives me the windowsill to hold "stuff" that I can get to when in my wheelchair. Thank you, Amazon, for letting me find some baskets that fit just right so I can be a little organized.

My friends and colleagues near and far want to help in some way. Against my requests to please not send anything, (I've got support and Amazon), gift baskets arrive. And arrive. While the "food" is less than edible at rehab I would not be able to go through all this booty in the months I will be here (never mind the sugar rush).

So, I pick through my gifts for things I can store here that I would enjoy. Items that need to be refrigerated when opened, rich dips and crackers that will not go with my apple juice cups, and items too large are put to the side. Some I can send home with the 'rents. The rest? Here comes Santa, or as my friend put it, Vito Corleone.

I sort the treats by sugar content and taste. I start to make small piles strategically placed in my room. Then the favor granting begins.

My MFA is young. She often works double shifts doing something I could never do. I admire her, and she treats me well. I size her up and she seems the healthy kind of gal. I ask her if she likes granola and protein bars – some made with real chocolate. She pauses and says yes. I tell her I am blessed by these gifts and want to share, go ahead, and take this pile off my hands. I reiterate she works long and hard and I can see how tired she is. I think she needed in her words "a little somethin' somethin'" but she is unsure, I can only surmise because the elderly patients don't see her as I do, and she is not used to acts of kindness and gratitude. She finally takes the stash and says thank you. I get 3 apple juices with my next tray.

I am learning the aides and how to interact with each one. Not that I am not generally polite, but I am becoming sickly sweetly nice. "I am sorry to bother you… thank you soooo much…. I appreciate your help…. I'm trying to do as much as I can as I know you are busy…" part of me truly thinks this way, another part knows you get more with honey.

Several residents are required to walk throughout the day. As such they make it down to my end of the hall. As I roll along the halls, I tap an arm, and whisper, "come see me, I got goodies". The residents between 65 and 80 often lament that there is not an evening snack available. They mention how other places will come by @7pm with "just a taste". Here 7 pm begins the witching hour. The residents are all "put away" for the evening. I can understand the need for structure and schedules. They need to get residents changed and settled in bed; the nurses make their rounds as well. You can't have 40 people roaming the halls. (Ok in reality it's more like sitting in the halls or day room). I am allowed to stay up in my room as long as I want, but honestly my time is somewhere between 8-9. I stay up but feel better getting my booboo body into the bed.

The visits begin. They walk and stop by and say hey. We share a snack and I send them back with something for later. A single cookie goes a long way. Now when I roll along people move to the side, I don't have to worry about navigating around. I am getting gossip and weather reports. I am not building my crew as much as I am "rolling" them over. Other residents are going home much more quickly than I will. New residents take their place. This is the circle of life here.

I was also given a gift of low sodium seasoning. I am just stopping short of placing a teaspoon in baggies to distribute. Naw, I am not that kind of dealer.

PATIENT ZERO

We have heard that while my injuries are severe, they are not the worst of any resident here. Continually people speak of a young construction worker who had everything from his hips down shattered. He was a resident for a year. I cannot wrap my head around living here for that long a period.

He is a legend. He is the worst injury to walk out of this place. He is Paul Bunyan, George Washington, and Dirty Harry all in one. He comes back to see the therapists who changed his life, who he feels is family.

I can see how you can feel strongly for these strangers. After only 2 weeks here I knew about my therapists' families, their plans for the weekend and dilemmas about flooring while moving to a new home among other things. We talk Walking Dead and having kids in college. There is a Harry Chapin song where he sings about "let time go lightly". That's what they do for their patients, while being with you at your worst and pushing you they let time go lightly. This is not a job for any of them, this is a calling. They speak with a love of what they do like they were making a million dollars. I can't imagine what separation I will feel at the end of my journey. How can you thank someone for guiding you to a second chance?

Back to patient zero. I had a glimpse of him once before but thought he may be a 4th floor resident (long term). While I know I shouldn't have, I couldn't help but stare at his leg which has seen better days. He saw me look and smiled. He has been where I am now, new to this life and still a little shell shocked. This is the first time I thought people will be looking at me when I get out. Wheelchair/walker/limp. No matter how much I progress there will be a long period that others will see me as broken. I'll cross that bridge when I come to it.

He was back today, but I saw him walk in on crutches, backpack casually slung over his shoulders and a backwards baseball cap. It was like Norm from Cheers walked in. He sat down and started to gossip. I asked my PT is this "the guy?" She states yes. Every time he has a doctor's appointment in the area, he comes in. Every time. The positive energy coming off this guy charged the room and it's contagious! He lives up to the legend.

PS: multiple send-offs as 3 patients were going home the next day. I was there for one of my crew's dance party. Despacito today. Toe tapping and hand clapping. One pt told me shake it – I asked her is she crazy? I want to get out of here not shatter this ass tablet! Laughter and goodbyes.

SO, I TEND TO CUSS

The English language is marvelous, if you forget the i before e except after c and then the shit ton of other words that don't follow that either.

See that? I typed shit. Sometimes cuss words just work their way into your day-to-day conversations like that. They can diminish you, say if you used them during a job interview or meeting the queen, or they can enhance your narrative. Case in point, let's study the f-bomb:

Hit your thumb with a hammer?

Loud resounding f-bomb!!!!

Talking with a clueless individual?

You don't know what the f-bomb you are talking about.

Just heard your favorite musician died.

Awww, f-bomb.

Having some asswipe not watch where he is driving and change your life forever?

F-bomb f-bomb f-bomb

PT not only stands for physical therapist, but for pain and torturer. To work, you have to be pushed beyond what is easy. No pain no gain, (although if I hear that one more time I may hurl).

My therapist that makes me "walk" for coffee has me out for my daily shuffle. Every day a little more, a little further. We go into the hall, practice turning which is not my strong point. I continually am Ross from Friends as I pivot, pivot. That is wrong, easy, but wrong. Quick, but wrong. You have to make approximately 17 micro steps to turn safely. God grant me patience.

He has me make my coffee, reach in the fridge to get milk (baby container). Open the milk, add it to my coffee, put the milk back, close the fridge. He hands me a spoon. I lift my brow and he says stir. I say no thanks I don't use a spoon. He says today you do.

As he holds my coffee, I look for the quickest route back to my wheelchair. He looks the long way. My shoulders slump and I sigh "f-bomb".

He stops, looks and bursts out laughing. Then he says he wanted to see my reaction and just head back. I apologize but explain he must get used to it the more I become "me" again.

WE'RE NOT IN KANSAS...

Or Florida for that matter. Baby it's cold outside and in. 50 degrees for someone who has been living down south for ~22 years is cold.

I couldn't sleep at all last night. I decided to Netflix binge. By midnight I gave in and asked for a pain pill. Aside from when I have therapy, I have only been taking Tylenol for about 5 days, and pain meds sporadically before then. I have a long recovery and I know the more I need and depend on these pills the more difficult it will become to not use them. The PA reminded me I am only in rehab 2 weeks and told me don't be a hero.

In my mind? I'm no hero, I'm an Avenger. I'm Ironman. Or Titanium

Woman.

During a middle of the night check, I chat with MFA #2. Cookies are exchanged. I will have a shower before the daily grind begins. My right side feels like the entire thing has a charley horse. The night nurse when she sees I'm still up recommends other Netflix shows. I tell her I'll add them to the list as I will be here awhile.

5:40 am and we pack up for the shower room. As it's "my day off" I grab my Walking Dead pj pants because that is how I classify myself. Later the nurse will have to put on the torture stockings to help reduce the inflammation, rolling up the pjs will be the easier way for her to do so.

The shower room was an icebox. Turns out a window was stuck in the open position. She couldn't unstick it, and as for me, well the ability to not be able to stand makes this a task for another day. We figure out let's just put the water on hot and go from there. Please take a moment to appreciate your last shower. How easy it is to just stroll in and stand and shower. Drop something? Just bend and pick it up. Revel in the little things.

If you can't experience it, it is difficult to explain living in a wheelchair in a rehab center. There is a very funny English comedian Michael McIntyre that does a routine about people with and without children. If you haven't seen it, I implore you watch it now. It is laugh out loud funny. While it is not the same, I think it will let you see the similarities about how different the same situation can be from two varying perspectives.

Shower is done, body dried, clothes thrown on and back to my room. And to…my new favorite amazon purchase, my blow dryer. MFA #2 plugs it in and closes the door. I have not been able to dry my hair in 26 days. I pleasantly sigh. I left it plugged in as I wasn't sure if I would turn it on later that day to feel the warmth again.

I got back into bed —— drum roll please —— all by myself.

It wasn't quick or pretty but was a task full of satisfaction. I had been practicing. By the time John comes for a visit I will have a host of party tricks to show off. I was tired. It was 6:30 and I needed a nap. The 2 hours of sleep I did get was not enough.

Up for breakfast (which was a little disappointing that am, ended up hitting the snack baskets). In my chair, I talked with John, checked FB, and watched HGTV.

One of the residents walking with his walker stops by my room. He is an elderly Indian gentleman whose English is rough. We generally smile, wave and exchange basic pleasantries. This day he talks. He knows my crew of the under 80 crowd all went home yesterday. He cajoles me to wheel out to the hall to sit in the sun by the window. A half hour he stated. You need to get out of your room for half an hour. Sit and be warm. Look out the window. He walked up and down several more times to make sure I am not retreating to my sanctuary. I explain to him while there is no therapy today, I still work in my room. These muscles betray me as soon as they think no one is watching. They need to know I am always watching. Stretch, move, bend. Even 1/2 an inch. There is no rest for the weary.

He was right. The sun felt good on my busted body. While my room and its window overlooked a parking lot and a garbage container was if I positioned my wheelchair just right, I didn't see the junk. My view was from a different perspective.

BALLET BARRE, NOT THE TYPE OF BAR I AM USED TO

I am sure you have all seen on tv or heard about athletes doing ballet to enhance their performance. Often the joke shows them struggling at the barre. Let me tell you my friends, the struggle is real.

There are only so many exercises you can do while balancing on one leg and holding onto your walker, wheelchair &/or therapist for dear life. Now I "walk" to the hall which has a barre on about 30 feet of wall. I stood tall, held on until my knuckles were white, and moved this currently unresponsive leg a few inches hither and yon. Stretch and the muscle memory will get jump started. I'd say it was successful as I went from having someone move the leg to being able to move it several inches in different directions myself.

Then my OT says new exercise. I am to hold onto the barre and take sideways "steps". I can only surmise he started doing drugs. How do you walk sideways on one leg? And why the hell do I want to?

He tells me because some day I will go home. Someday I will need to get out of this chair and get on a seat in an airplane. Even with an aisle seat I will need to "scootch" over. I will need to do it safely.

Dramatic pause as he mentions going home.

Let's do it. He demonstrates not once but three times. I try. I swear. I sweat. He wants 7 steps. I do it. 4,5,6, 7…I go 10.

But wait, I need to go back the other way. F-bomb.

6,7,8 – I couldn't. I asked for the chair. My forehead rested against the cool stone wall as I held on. I was spent. The barre is my nemesis.

Ballerinas are badass in my book now.

He has to wheel me back into the therapy room. I was given a towel. I was drenched in sweat and all I wanted to do was sleep. Nope. Weight training first. I honestly can't understand what the hell just happened. He says every time I try something new, I struggle. But then I surpass my record after that. We will do this every other day. We will do this for weeks. Because someday I will go home, and I will be ready.

SOCIALIZATION IS NEEDED AS PART OF THE HEALING PROCESS

I go to therapy 2x a day. In between I do additional exercises in my room. I also practice things like putting on shoes and socks or getting in and out of my bed.

I have access to the internet (mostly) and get visitors (limited by my choice at that point). I have Netflix and Direct TV. I have extra time to try and level up on Toy Blast. I exchange pleasantries with the residents. I believed I had ample socialization.

I stay far away from the day room if I can avoid it. My therapy sessions are scheduled at the same time as the "recreational events". I am the youngest resident, and the plight of the others cannot help but bring you down. I am fighting uphill both ways and can't afford to sink into a depression.

The recreational staff and others continued to mention I stay in my room and don't engage. I bite my tongue most times, other times my mouth just runs. I tell them I can't. I am at war. Every day, every movement, every ounce of my strength needed to be focused on walking out of there. I can't be part of the malaise and despair that is in that room, in those halls.

I had staff come see me. There is a "special dinner" – will I RSVP yes? There will be music. It's a Big Secret. They will not say what was being served, give details on the entertainment or the reason for the shindig. They just keep stating I shouldn't stay in my room. Other residents ask me will I be going? I give in. I'll do it – once.

I asked what time the party is. Five. But you have to be ready to go at 4:30. Remember they have to get the attendees all down in 2 elevators. Wheelchairs, walkers, and all. I am trying to rest when they come for me @4. Rush rush rush, we need to go. I sigh and get in my chair.

These events must be big for the residents. I am one of the last to arrive

1/2 hour early and all the good seats were already taken. Would I like to sit with the lady in the pink sweater (whose eyes are closed)? I waited for my other option. Or would I like a table by myself? Winner winner chicken dinner.

My cruise director came to discuss the menu. Eggplant or some kind of steak. I glanced around at the food. I told them the steak and garlic potatoes - with nothing. No gravy, nothing. Without the oily toppings that I can only assume are put on to lubricate the food so you can swallow without chewing I might have had a chance.

The "entertainment" began. I will call him Tony Goombah. He had a microphone and a small BOOM box that connected to the speaker system. Sinatra and other classics. He was loud and off key, but I know he thinks he is Elvis. The whistling is worse than the singing. He is ON!

Company is brought over. My dining companion wants to be here less than I do. She is also hard of hearing and a low talker. Shoot me now. My food comes. It's wrong. They look and tell me it's wrong. Stare off – off to get me a new plate. Like my last visit to the dining room, I have nothing to drink. Uggghh.

They brought my food back and I took a small bite. It is garlic held together by paste. I tried to get someone's attention to get a drink. No go. I disengage the brakes on my chair as I prep to go in search of something wet. The aides descend upon me. Code Red – this is the Hotel California-you can never leave.

I give up and my mouth just goes, politely, but still. I may have said something along the lines of "May I please have a drink as this food is so dry, I need something to wash it down my throat so I don't choke."

Would I like a coke? ***coke = no name cola***

Does it have sugar, I asked? It's a special dinner, so yes. "Coke it is" my baby half can is placed on the table. I actually got 2. For meals we get silverware, except tonight with steak we get plastic forks and knives. My companion can't cut the steak. I couldn't get to her dish. Brakes off the wheelchair and help arrived. She mumbled if we can't cut it how is she to chew?

Tony G. finishes – thanks for coming to his show see you next time. Fat chance in hell.

My companion wants to leave. Just get her to the lobby. She knows the drill. The line will form, and we will never make it upstairs. The aides ignore her plea. I got this. She tells me get the aide in red. Off I go. I roll by and tell her the lady is pissed and she should go get her – all as I continue on to the lobby. I am 4th in line.

We are done and back by 6:05. It was exhausting. Tonight, I get ready for bed with no help. Toilet, wash, change, dirty clothes in the hamper and off I go to bed. With one stop. I need something sweet to cap off my wonderful meal. I look at the box and laugh. I take it as a good sign. Its Walkers Brand Cookies.

THE NEVER-ENDING ASSESSMENTS

I get more assessments and reports than a child in daycare. Again, I do as asked. Except once.

When your ass tablet is shattered any incorrect movement will re-shatter it. There is not much room to try and fix it again should something happen. My initial days here required the use of a medieval torture device called an abduction pillow. To stabilize my hips a pillow (no illustration does justice to how bad it is, nor the level of effort required to use it) is strapped to and between both of your legs. To do so requires 2 people. Any movement hurts. Once strapped in then the 2 people turn you on your side. I would have an anxiety attack and cry more often than not when this was needed to be done. This was done several times throughout the day and night. My 10 days stay in the hospital had already caused pressure sores.

This task was my inspiration (after coffee) to be able to get myself out of bed, in my chair and ultimately (Yeah!) to the bathroom.

The pillow remains in my room (in case of emergency) but I have regulated IT to the corner. It will never be part of my life again. Until the PT tells me she has to see if I can roll (with help) to either side. NO. Not going to happen. She gently states she will not hurt me, and she needs to see if I can do it.

Just check the No box. The answer is NO. Anxiety sets in and she says ok, another day. Yesterday was that day.

The pain is minimal this time, but the anxiousness is higher. There is only her to help me vs the two people I am used to. My arm strength is much better. I reach for the rails of the bed and on 3 pull with all my might. Going down sucks. Repeat for the other side. She keeps a steady cadence to her voice talking me through precautions, how I will be able to turn eventually and that she has me. We are done. She smiles and says that's all she needed to see, and we are done.

I hate that f'ing pillow. I try to maintain positive energy for my healing but just the sight of this thing turns me to Mr. Hyde. I have never hated an inanimate object more. When the time comes, I need to find the best way to destroy this. I need to find a way to utterly destroy it the way it did me in the beginning. Suggestions welcome.

TAKE 5 MINUTES OUT OF YOUR DAY TODAY AND WORK WITH ME

I will say this until my last breath and believe it as much the first time or the 1,000th. Rehab is hard, it is pushing yourself beyond what you think is possible. You rethink all of the little things that you previously took for granted.

So today I am asking you for 5 minutes of your time – whenever it works for you in your day. I want you to follow along on just one of the rehab exercises.

Strength, balance, muscle memory. This is my mantra. Everything I do requires one or all of those three. My life is learning how to adapt safely.

I roll up to a table. On it is a pedal exerciser. Instead of pedaling with your feet, you strap your hands to either side and "pedal".

I've got this. I've used this before. The therapist sets the tension, puts 14 minutes on the clock, and I grip onto the handles and do 7 minutes forward and 7 minutes back. Not this time.

He raises the table. OT commands "Stand." Day by day I seriously am thinking he may be mentally ill or enjoying recreational Drugs.

I stand from the chair. Flamingo stance engaged. Now, he says, 8 minutes forward 7 minutes back. Notice too that he added a minute. If I need, I may sit in between.

Prior to the BOOM I was not the most coordinated person. The list of stupid falls and injuries goes on and on. This is just crazy.

So, for the audience participation part of today's program. Figure out something to do with your hands to keep them moving. Now stand. On one leg. Try it for only 5 minutes. If you put your other foot down, you just re-shattered your hip and you lose big time. Go. Curious how you did.

Progress Report on the Cupid Shuffle: 15 steps to the left, 15 steps to the right.

BAD DAYS ARE INEVITABLE

I've been on a streak. Every day I have surpassed the previous. As part of my afternoon therapy my leg and side gets massaged. Not the "this is so tranquil massage I should do this more often" but the "I will try and remember to breathe as every muscle is crying" as I cringe through the pain. This is necessary. Swelling continues, and the muscles are so tight they feel like stone. A good portion of my right side will have no movement until the end of eight weeks. The therapist has to release these muscles so someday I will be able to use them to walk again. The best part? When she stops.

Yesterday afternoon I was on the therapy table, and then I was off (in the air- not on the floor) when she touched my knee. The pain was searing. Everyone looked up in shock. She stated she barely touched me. The knee is swollen and hot. Inflammation at level 100. We try and figure out what happened.

Health background. I have 2 forms of autoimmune arthritis for which I see a rheumatologist. Unfortunately, I was told by the surgeon that I cannot take my primary current meds as it will interfere with the healing of the bone.

We think this may be a flare. They are very painful. Calls to the nurse while I am iced to try and reduce the swelling. Upstairs I go. I work with the nurse. She calls the PA. I get lidocaine patches, ice, and I ask for painkillers. I now need them for both knees.

Then a lightbulb goes off. I had been prescribed compression stockings to reduce the swelling. We now think because of the stockings the water/swelling congregated at the knees. I tell her we just traded one problem for another. I will now be declining the stockings.

I also have discomfort (not pain per se) where my leg attaches to my body. AKA the injury site. The therapists say it is normal. As I am standing more doing my Karate Kid Crane style exercises gravity is now pulling the bad side down.

Today we will work around the pain. There is no rest. I may not go forward these next few days, but I won't go back either.

VIRTUAL OPEN HOUSE

I am blessed. A statement you may not expect from someone in my current situation.

I continue to get inquiries on what do I need, what can someone send? Space is at a premium. I have figured how to adapt to my temporary home.

I thought perhaps I will walk you through my digs so you can understand why I turned down your offers.

Spoiler alert. The rehab center is old. I am not here for aesthetics – I am here to learn to walk again, and the therapists are 5 Star. It is clean, and they clean everything every day. The daily living care and "lifestyle" are on the opposite end of where I would place myself. Yet I can't have one without the other.

When I get out of bed and into the chair there is a view to the door. There is a closet to the left. I have now put my laundry bag inside and have a few things hanging. Not that I can hang anything up, but I can pull them down. It is not convenient, but I use it. This place is all about how to go back to living your life and zero about being easy. To the right is the bathroom.

To use either of these I have to navigate the wheelchair. Try turning in this cramped space. Also, I do not have a roommate today, but note this is a shared room.

Live tours can be scheduled with an appointment. Unfortunately, the therapy room is off limits. To respect the privacy of the residents and the hard work that goes on there I totally agree.

My Spot

Being in a wheelchair my access to things right in front of me is limited. I still have precautions of things I cannot do (like bend, lean, etc.) due to my injury. My spot is in my wheelchair, between the window (where I have baskets on the sill) and the bed (where I have my adaptive tools). I have to back in. My wheelchair did not fit until I pushed the bed over, which was not as easy as it sounds. As I back in inch by inch I hold onto the tray table and drag it with me. I do this several times a day. I can see the TV and look out the window.

More things I can't reach

The side table is beside the bed behind me and not really accessible. The walker needs to stay by the bed to let me transfer to the wheelchair. The phone is on the table – so useless. John "MacGyvered" a phone charger. It is tied to the bed with the same bakery string I use to turn on/off the lights.

The rest of my crap

I can't bend, even in the chair. I can't use the "spacious" 2 Draws I have easily. I have figured out how to adapt to my temporary home. Clothes are in there. Everything else I need is on top. My snacks, extra towels (I sweat like a mother at therapy – I am washing up multiple times a day). Some of my adaptive tools I don't need all throughout the day (the other tools are always within reach in the bed or table). A sweatshirt for the days I go outside. THAT pillow. And whatever the nurses and aides decide to throw for the day, on the dresser, on the chairs, sometimes on the end of the bed.

By the way that makes me crazy. This is my temporary home. Then they come in and just drop crap all over the place. It's not malicious it's just easy for them.

My office

So to make the most of my space, have access to what I need, and be able to charge my phone and iPad, I back in to the side of my bed by the window. I pull the "dinner" tray with me to set my stuff. I can see the TV and look out the window.

MY OWN BONFIRE OF THE VANITIES AND OTHER HUMBLING THINGS

Flashback to my rehab life before showers. Once I was strong enough to be in the wheelchair for a limited amount of time, I was able to request to go to the "salon". I desperately needed my hair washed. DESPERATELY.

"The Girl" comes once a week and you have to get your name on the list. I do so. When the day comes, it is late afternoon when they call for me. Upstairs we go. I have only heard about upstairs.

The lay of the land here:

- 1st floor dining room, admin offices, reception, therapy room, maintenance, and storage

- 2nd floor rehab residents, some offices, day room and a little garden

- 3rd floor is dementia residents, "salon", day room

- 4th floor, long term residents same set up as 2nd floor sans garden

When I get upstairs residents line the hall. You can look in their faces and see no one is there. Sadness starts to overtake you. They continue to wheel me and place me "on the line" in the hall. Anxiety sets in.

The ladies (also in the hall) are in varying stages of hair coloring, drying (old fashion Dryer covering you head), curlers, etc. Think Steel Magnolias geriatric edition.

The girl is in her late 40s, early 50s. Stereotypical stylist. She asks what I need. Just shampoo and condition please. I do not want to even stay here 5 extra minutes to get my hair dried.

As she works on 4 people at a time I notice when complete they all look the same. This is like an Alfred Hitchcock movie. I'm up.

The salon is actually a closet with a sink and a few shelves. The doorway is narrow. My wheelchair does not fit through. I am ready to cry again as I need clean hair. She jams me in. The next day I had maintenance repair my wheelchair. When asked what happened I say I have no idea.

I can not lean backwards. She places what looks like a dog collar on me that has a hose in the back that drains into the sink. Give my story, get hair washed, pay the lady and out to go back to my 2nd floor sanctuary. She only does assisted facilities and rehab centers. If this place was any indication, she racks up the $$$$ and will be able to retire before me. As she waves me off, she says she is here when I need a color and a cut.

Present day. I got up, went to the bathroom, washed up, brushed my teeth, and got dressed. All by myself. It took an hour. I noticed the grey starting to take over. How much does it bother me? Actually, not at all.

My situation has caused me to cease to have any semblance of modesty. More strangers have seen my naked ass then if I mooned the George Washington Bridge during rush hour. But that is not why I don't care. I don't care because very strong women in my life had grey/white hair and they rocked it. I don't remember my grandmother without her silky white hair. When my sister had cancer, her hair grew back short and grey. Another friend who has kicked cancer's ass also has a salt and pepper 'do and she looks beautiful. When people look at me, I don't want them to see the chair or my grey hair. I want them to see strength just like those women had/have. I want them to see Ironman. They will see Ironman.

Which brings me to unexpected visitors. Several staff members have stopped me or come by my room. They wanted my story. I thought by this time they all knew my injuries. That's not what they wanted – they want my story. I give them the synopsis. More questions – they all refer back to my condition just 3 weeks ago vs. now. What happened?

I told them I can be angry at God or embrace that He is with me. I can be all woe is me or I can work my ass tablet off to get home. I can feel isolated and alone or understand how loved I am by the outpouring of prayers, positive energy, calls, texts, and junk food I get every day.

I can be a victim, or I can be Ironman. I think we all know what I choose.

SUNDAY MORNING BREAKFAST WITH THE LADIES

After my 6 am meds I am ready to tackle the day. Get up and head to the bathroom. Funny how simple that seems. My swollen leg makes me take 2x as long to move it off the bed. They measure inflammation by weighing you. They weigh your chair empty. Then you get wheeled onto the scale and they deduct the weight of the wheelchair. On bad days there has been a 16-pound variance one day to the next. So, I sit, wait for blood flow to resume, put a sneaker on, use walker, transfer to the chair. This process is getting mechanical to me.

Once done I decide to pick out my clothes and get my shower things together. When I'm ready I ring for the aide. Like a dog waiting on a bone, I ask for a shower. They have been incredibly short staffed. Yet I have been averaging 3 showers a week. When I can back at home, I will shower 2x a day just because I can.

The aide helps me Dress in the shower room. Wet surfaces and a broken ass tablet do not mix. Back to the room and my beloved blow Dryer.

Then the cleaning woman is here. Early. As there is no therapy today I have nowhere to go. I wheel myself to the day room to wait her out with my iPad. I told them I'm not staying and will have breakfast in my room. Then I am spotted by the ladies. ***sigh*** I wheel myself in. I take a spot away from everyone on the other side of the table. Nope. They point out if I sit there, I will be blocked in. Come on over. Introductions again. Every single time. They can not remember that we have met half a dozen times by now in addition to daily therapy. I smile like it's the first time. One woman smiles and laughs and calls me Candida. No, I say Candi. Candida?! No, C A N D I

Candida it is. Which I hate because it's a form of yeast infection. Hopefully they forget by tomorrow. Another woman rolls up. An Irish joke is made. Aha – a kindred soul. Conversations flow as best they can. What touches me is how they look out for each other. "S" has not eaten for 3 days. They try to get her to take little bites. "J" had a bad night because someone turned off the music which calms him. Who needs sweet and low? No one likes the eggs. (I already put my order in for cereal and pancakes).

The Irish lady forgot her radio. No music, and then she will not be able to listen to mass. Amazon music to the rescue and the Irish music flows. Calls to make it louder so "J" can hear. "S" is dancing in her chair. A few join in to sing Danny Boy. I look to my right and see my dining companion struggling. I take the brakes off and roll a little closer. I open her juice and she says thank you.

The ladies are bitching about the coffee. They need a good cup of tea with the music. No one helps them. They have been told they cannot have tea. Off I wheel to find MFA and tell her teas are requested. We all agree she is the best. "S" gets sad as she listens to a song that reminds her of Home. I changed the station. We are all good. As a reward I guess, I got 4 juices today. I had to cut the party short as I needed my 9ish meds and a restroom. I wave them off and tell them I will see them later. Or sometime in the next 5 weeks

I WISH I CAN MAKE MY BED

Really? With all going on with me what is the thought popping in my head? Aides come in daily and make my bed, change the sheets if need be and bring fresh towels. The cleaning lady washes the floor daily, empties the garbage and even puts a new roll of toilet paper on the holder (albeit backwards- age old debate). Sounds sweet – not so much.

My king-sized mattress is replaced by a hospital bed with rails that must be up as I am a fall risk. I don't like my feet tucked in the covers. I can't breathe. So every day I move my chair and tug at the hospital corners to free the blankets. I try – unsuccessfully every time – to arrange the pillows so I am comfortable. If they slip, I must raise the hospital bed, pull myself up, use my pony strap to move Meg-Leg, grab the walker, transfer to the wheelchair, use my grabber, and try and fix the pillow. Then reverse. My injury still does not allow me to turn or bend certain ways. If I want to move the covers, I again have to use my adaptive tools and the skills of a rodeo wrangler.

I must sleep with my legs even with my hip. I cannot cross my legs. I can't sleep on my side or my back. I slip down during the night, so I have to lower the head of the bed, grab the metal rails, and pull myself back as far as possible. Then try and adjust to be comfortable.

The heat is on as the weather has changed. It is ~78* in my room. I sweat. I try opening the windows to offset the unbearable temperature. Then I am freezing as the wind kicks in. I give up and call the aide at 2 am to please close the window.

I miss my bed, my covers, my pillow, and being able to sleep on my belly under the fan. I miss being able to turn around easily and adjust the pillow. I miss not having to wrangle the sheets, so my feet are free.

As much as I miss and yearn for all of these things, I miss my family even more. Two weeks until John comes

HOW YOU SEE YOURSELF VS. HOW OTHERS SEE YOU

If I had to describe myself right now, I would say picture one big muscle ache. That smells slightly of sweat. And needs a haircut.

If I were to describe my progress, I would say life changing. The weight lifted off my shoulders when I truly believed I would not be confined to this chair that defines freedom.

Yet what do others think? Should I care for that matter? I knew just by looking at their faces what everyone in the hospital thought as there was no hiding behind a facade. Here, now, I push forward a positive attitude. Fake it 'til you make it? Partly. The quicker I get everyone off the pity train the quicker it can leave the station – without me.

The offers for visits are still abundant, yet I am still not there. Will I be still in this chair? I honestly don't know. Even if I give 1/10th of 1% of my energy to try and make the visit less awkward that is still energy better utilized getting better.

The visitors I do have already knew me at some time in my life when I was broken, just not to this extent. I don't "try" for them but do perform some of my dog and pony show tricks like standing from my chair to keep them with me on my journey. They have earned to be part of this progress. There is still the errant tear (or tears), but they are fewer and farther between. You all know my daily struggles, but you don't have to witness it firsthand to support me. If this happened 20 years ago, I am not sure I would be doing so well. The ability to call and text lets me be connected. Social media keeps me in the loop.

I am not sure how others really see me now, or how they will in the future. I think it's more important how I see myself.

I GOT INTO A CAR TODAY

Occupational therapy is getting you ready for real life. That includes getting back in a car. Next to rehab that's the last place I want to be.

We have to practice car transfers. How can you get in and out safely. Could I even get in or out at this point. Going to the doctor, to the airport, Home and eventually outpatient therapy means cars are in my future. Like everything we have to figure out how can I do things.

Jacket on. Walker to get up. I look and my chair is being left behind. I am to walk out of the therapy room, into the parking lot, down a small incline to the car. When measured it is 150 feet. It might as well be a mile. There is no sitting and resting in between. I can sit when I get to the car. My arms are aching (I already did weight training prior to our little stroll). My leg where it attaches to my body feels like it is held on by string that is unraveling. That is the magic of gravity. The more I stand the more the leg pulls down. These muscles that will not be worked for 8 weeks don't know what to do. I can pause and then start again. But during that pause I am still standing on one leg (toe touch with the Meg-leg) and use my arms to hold me up on the walker. A pause gives little relief.

Finally, near the car. As I struggle a visitor is pulling up to ask us where she can park as the lot is full. Really? Do I look like the f'ing parking lot attendant? I'm a little busy. She tries to turn and again I think this is how I die. Get through all of this and an idiot is going to run me over in the rehab lot.

The OT tells me to stay. Where the hell does he think I am going to run off to? He moves his wife's car (which he took because he thought I needed the little bit of height) up and directs me the easy 27 moves it will take to get in. The PT shows up. She was late today. Thanks for coming, I tell her and smile.

In the car and anxiety rises. The car is off. Ok I'm done. I want out. I need out. He reminds me I have to walk back up the incline. I am ready to nap. I have to learn how to reach to put on the seatbelt. I close my eyes and breathe. I am done. I will crawl back to not be in this car.

I'm out and the air fills my lungs, and I am ok. Then I look at Everest before me. Step, step, step, step, pause. Repeat multiple times. I can see my room from here. I do this for 146 feet and tell them to get the chair I can't make it the last 4. I noticed another resident doing a car transfer. The car was pulled up close to the door. I look at the OT and call him a bastard. He reminds me I said push me to get back to my life. Then he smiles and pats me on the back. We will do this a few more times with other cars over the next few weeks. He tells me if I can't get home for Thanksgiving I will get a pass for the day – because I will be able to get in a car by then.

At PT in the afternoon, I walk another 150+ feet indoors. At the end of the stretching exercises, I called uncle. I tell her please no more. She gives me both heat and ice therapy this session in addition to the deep muscle (pain) massage to try and loosen this leg that feels like stone. She tells me she was up in the night; she didn't know why. But she started thinking about changes she will make with my therapy. She thought I should know I was in her thoughts.

I am already feeling the loss of these people weeks before I will be leaving here. I cannot fathom them not being part of my life after they are working so hard to give mine back to me.

Mr. B left today. He came in with his son with tears in his eyes to thank everyone and was cheered out like he scored the winning touchdown. Mr. L will leave Saturday. His wife and daughter let me know even though they speak no English. They all touched my shoulder at different times today and gave me the same message – "soon".

NOT EVERY DAY WILL BE INSPIRING, PHILOSOPHICAL OR FUN

Welcome to that day. Tried to get in a shower today, no luck. That should have set off a warning bell. OT was going well until he had me stand, and not hold onto the walker, and try and twist 2 inches in either direction. Epic failure. Time and time again. I couldn't. This is my next obstacle which is extremely hard for someone with no coordination. I need to be able to do this if I ever want to get rid of the walker (which is after I get rid of the chair). If I want to go in the kitchen and make my own coffee and need to turn and reach for a cup, I need to do this the OT states. I tell him I will hold onto the counter.

Issues with insurance and disability payments. Paperwork I would rather do without now. Disgusting food. My nap interrupted.

A call from my oldest son – this is what breaks me today. He has been affected more than he has let on. I am broken again, a feeling I have kept at bay. I cry alone in my room because all I want to do is hug my child. It will be a month before that is possible. He cannot take off from work and I cannot go home. I hate the driver. I cannot waste my energy on hate but as a mother I cannot help but have this feeling right now.

Tomorrow will be a better day.

SAID TODAY WOULD BE BETTER

Thank you for those who reached out in response to my bad day. I began journaling my experiences as an outlet to get the crazy out of my head. I write and share my thoughts so maybe someday this "guide" will help someone in my position navigate this journey. I stated in the beginning this will be open and honest, to do otherwise defeats the purpose. So, there will be bad days.

How do you get beyond the despair?

Put on your favorite Walking Dead pjs.

Eat peeps before breakfast.

Get a SHOWER- YEAH!!!!

Get a good breakfast from MFA – pancakes, real butter, and 3 kinds of juice.

Dust off my sorry ass, wear a t-shirt that makes me think of my son and get ready for the day and leave yesterday behind – because Ironman is back.

GENERALLY, THIS IS NOT A PLACE OF JOY

No one wants to be here. Life circumstances have placed every resident here. For some this will be the last place they will reside. Last week there were 2 deaths. The recreational team has small daily events geared to the elderly. They are escorted downstairs, and they get a break from the monotony of the day. Some pass the time by sitting in the halls. There is no life on the resident floors.

But oh Rehab! Rehab is about possibilities and hope and encouragement. The faces are changing, most of the people who were here when I started have gone home. Yet the people occupying these seats are somewhat interchangeable. Rehab is where we work. There is always music and an abundance of positive energy. The staff is like a family. They work well together and socialize outside of here. Today one of their own is leaving for another opportunity, so today they were doing Karaoke.

Fast forward to trying to get someone to sing. When they ask me, I simply state I don't see alcohol. I am told I don't need alcohol to sing. Yes, yes I do.

Mr. L is given the microphone. He starts singing in Korean (but think Karate Kid movies). He is on a roll and doesn't stop. They put on Cyndi Lauper, but he still sing the old Korean song to the beat of Girls Just Want to Have Fun. His wife shows up. She is beside herself at him singing. The room is enthralled – not because it's good but because there is life in the residents. It's also his last session – dance party. I am done but ask to stay. The song? Gangnam Style. His wife is killing it, the PT has him up. He is more dabbing but still – amazing for a guy in a walker. When it's over we clap and cheer.

As for me? Today I was able to bend my leg while lying down. I bent it without someone having to move it for me. The few inches made me sweat, grunt, and as always forget to breathe. I did sets of 5. Four sets of 5. Two days ago, I could not do one. There are other movements I still cannot do, but today I did this.

Told you – today would be a better day.

HALFWAY MARK AND A NEW SHORT-TERM GOAL

I have officially been a rehab resident for four weeks today. I am at the halfway mark of my surgeon's plan. It feels like yesterday and forever at the same time. Can I survive another four weeks away from home? Will four weeks be enough to prepare me for life away from these amazing therapists? The dichotomy of what the next four weeks holds has me spinning.

I am tired. Everything I do, every move I make takes so much energy – physically and emotionally. Everyday has a new challenge. Did I mention I am tired?

John will be here in a week. I am already planning. I will have a roommate on Monday (more on that tomorrow). The weather has turned cold and harsh. We will not be able to sit outside. We will not sit in the day room. That leaves us 1/2 of a shared hospital room or downstairs in Gen Pop. I need him. I need normal for a day.

I approached the PT and asked how I can get out of here for a day. I need a day pass. I cannot miss any therapy. My muscles mock me after my "day off" Sundays, and that is with me working in my room. I told her I need the pass for next Sunday – my off day. How can I make this happen?

Question answer period starts. Where am I going? With whom? What is the lay of the land? Will there be steps? I imagine for a moment if I had a daughter instead of sons. If some guy wanted to date my daughter, he would get the 3rd degree like this. That would still entail less questions than what I am put through.

I will need to go up a curb with crutches. I will need to walk on uneven ground with crutches. I will need to walk 150 feet without sitting (I can stop) with a walker, I will need to use the walker in the bathroom instead of the wheelchair. I will need to do more stairs with crutches. Finally, I will need someone to come and certify a car transfer (will nominate Pops and his minivan).

sigh should we add jumping jacks to that list? Well guess what?

- Curb – done

- Walked back through the parking lot (uneven ground on an incline) from the curb ~200 feet – done

- 150 feet with the walker – done

- Walker in the bathroom – done done done

- Stairs – TEN today. Up, rest, then down – DONE MF!

Car transfer will be next week. Traveling with me will be like going out with a newborn, I come with a lot of stuff. Walker, crutches, transfer chair. A few other odds and ends. Now starts the coordination. I have a week. Stay tuned.

SURVIVING IN REHAB IS A LITTLE LIKE BEING IN JAIL

Your every move is monitored, they do a bed check, you can't leave anytime you want, hell you can't even get in an elevator by yourself. You are at the mercy of others. The food – I'm not even going to go there. So how do you flourish never mind survive?

I've been doing the trade for favors thing – thanks to many of you who have sent me more things than I have room for or could ever possible use/eat. Granola bars got me an early am shower, a coloring book got me 6 juices, cookies for the residents made navigating the halls in my wheelchair easier. But my biggest coup to date? The roommate situation.

Due to a really bad thing that happened here I was moved to the primo room at the end of the hall. My then roommate was moved upstairs to floor 3 – enough said. I have been surprisingly by myself. Then one of the admin staff on this floor came to speak with me. Turns out her mother is having a knee replacement and will be a fellow resident. She has a say in room assignments and has been trying to keep the bed open for her mom. She says I am a nice person and worries that her mom will be placed with someone who is not as together as she is. If I agree.

Of course! To disagree would most likely get me a 90-year-old dementia patient. How do I make this a win/win?

We have a heart-to-heart talk away from everyone in my room. I tell her the therapists are amazing, but she needs to watch for her mom on the floor. I understand they are shorthanded, and now that I can get around in my chair, I can manage most things. But her mom will need help, especially in the beginning.

We discuss which aides are great (perhaps she can help with their assignments?). We discuss nurses and medication (sometimes I have to go down the hall to get my meds before therapy). The talk goes on for about 1/2 an hour. We will exchange cell numbers next week when her mom moves in – just in case. She will be with her mom after her shifts are done as a family member but will also be able to pop in during the day to make sure everything is ok. Me and B are going to be besties for my last few weeks.

As for me today? My ass tablet is sore and swollen today. The weather and exercise done did me in. I am heading to bed for some binge watching of mindless tv as I continue to plot world domination.

MY NAKED ASS TABLET

My broken ass tablet is sore. I can't categorize it as pain as I now equate pain with the first days of the BOOM. It is uncomfortable, annoying, sore, bothersome - I can keep going. It feels swollen to me. I can't tell as I still can't turn and look. I talk to the therapist, and we decide I'll take it easy the rest of the weekend. "This is expected" "It's the cold" I keep hearing these phrases. How do they know? Anyone here ever break an ass tablet? My fear is always that something is wrong, and I will be going backwards. I have been poked and prodded and told I am ok – but how do they really know?

Late last night I finally gave in and asked for a painkiller. It's not something I do often (aside from therapy) but I know rest is key to my recovery. Sleep was just ok last night; I was up and down several times. When morning came, I asked for a shower.

Today's aide is one I haven't had for a bit – when she was helping me, she said "Wow". Obviously, that got my attention. Wow what? She said she can't believe how well my incision has healed. Then she leans in to take a closer look. I stand and turn slightly to give her a better view of the hip and backside. She again tells me how good it looks. As she saw me at the worst, I told her how uncomfortable I am, and ask what does she think? Rest today – is her answer. They all know how hard I am working. Ok, shower done, back to the room.

The nurse comes by for my morning vitals check and meds. How are you today? Well, since you are asking, I try and get another opinion on my ass tablet. In my room I drop my shorts. She then wants to see the other side for comparison. The verdict? Rest today. She will make a note for the doctor to come by tomorrow to make me feel better.

You know what would make me feel better? To be able to bend and pick something up. To sleep in a bed without handrails. To be able to walk on 2 feet. Maybe ice cream.

A BRIEF PSA INSPIRED BY MY LLBFF

For years now my LLBFF has been sending sporadic, random, inspirational messages in the am to which I usually have some wise ass retort.

Today she sent me something about faith and the fact that while we may not understand, events in our life are not random. There is something to be learned.

I responded I can't wait to figure out what I'm supposed to be learning.

She responded quickly "I think there are lots of things. Your strength in adversity. Learning to conquer fear. Repairing broken relationships."

She is one of my champions. She has seen me beyond broken and lauds every accomplishment no matter how small. While I talk about my "walking" she reacts like WALKING! She pushes me to give myself credit. She cries with me. Her presence in my life, beyond this tragic BOOM (smiling for you K) has been a constant for ~28 years and I know her friendship is a gift not many people will ever have in their life.

And she brought me ice cream yesterday.

I have a league of champions I will never be able to thank enough. I have a family whose heart beats with mine even over a thousand miles away. While I am still learning what this journey is about, for right now I know how blessed I am.

Keith Urban wrote a love song for his wife about how she saved him. The first part of the song describes my life from September 19th through today. For everyone supporting me, that song now has a special meaning.

PS: my last response to this morning's text? What else I am learning? Sent her a picture of the karate kid doing the crane technique.

THE STATE OF ELDER CARE

You all understand I am basically in a nursing home. What have I learned? The elderly blend into the woodwork. People speak in front of residents with no filter because 99.9% don't or can't follow along. I am experiencing firsthand a for profit center that is continually understaffed as they run lean. They have no contingency plan should they need even 1 more body. They supplement staff by the use of per diem workers that they contract for 12 hour shifts to eliminate overtime and benefits.

The support staff falls into 2 categories; those who truly care but are being burned out by trying their best to cover residents' needs, and those who basically can't give a F'. They have learned how to game the system and there is no consequences to their actions.

I want to point out before I continue, I am not in some shit hole place. It is older and worn and the renovations they are doing are more lipstick on a pig than substantive. However, the rehab is 5 Star and they do not skimp on the therapy. The place is thoroughly cleaned top to bottom every day. The recreation department does little events every day to break up the monotony of being here.

***if you are over the age of 80 you may appreciate the events ***

But the longer I am a resident the more I am seeing and hearing. I have been blessed by the rate of my recovery even though it will be quite some time before I am able to walk on my own. As such if no one answers the call button for my meds, I roll down to the nurse to get them administered. I have taken to going in the hall and grabbing clean towels in the am to have in my room. When I am getting frustrated by the lack of response to my needs I now wheel to the nursing admin office and block the door with my extra wide wheelchair and put the brakes on. No one goes in or out until someone helps me. I have relationships with aides that help to get a shower or extra juice. I have a great support system that keeps me fed with real food in addition to the pleasure of their company. I tell the staff when I don't agree with any medical change.

In a nutshell I can advocate for myself. Yet I am surrounded by those that cannot and as bad as some of my bad days are, theirs are worse. My 3 showers a week is a luxury compared to some of their schedules. Their call buttons are eventually answered but that does not mean the reason they rang the bell is addressed in what I would deem a reasonable timeframe. I am past the 1/2-way mark of my stay. With the exception of 1 gentleman there is no one left in therapy with me from when I started. For the elderly rehab patients whose time is transient no one has to listen to their woes. For the long-term patients, they try not to rock the boat, which I understand. I have uttered the phrase "I have to live here. I am not going to piss off the people who are here day to day that I must rely on" multiple times to family and friends who are astonished at some of the crap I deal with. I say that while knowing my stay is only two months. I cannot fathom if this were my life. May that never be my future.

PERSPECTIVE

Today I was up from 5:15. All I could think of is I need a shower. After the shift change, I ring the call button around 7:30. Timing is everything. I need to get my shower in before they have to get the other residents ready for breakfast, or else I have to wait until after 9:30. That is very close to my am therapy which means it will most likely not happen today. The nurse on duty comes in rather than the aide. She says people are running late but she will make sure she gets someone.

Minutes later there is a commotion in the hall. One of the residents a few doors down is coding. There's more staff running up the stairs than I have ever seen in one place since I've been here. Calls for the doctor and 911. As much as I strain to hear I can't figure out who it is. Sounds of the ambulance are too far away for my liking. Time is again going slower. Yelling to check for a DNR order. I think I hear them saying what I have come to know as the Filipino affection of grandpa. I now know who this is. My heart is saddened along with the staff standing outside my door who look forlorn.

The ambulance is here. Everything is quiet, too quiet. The silence is broken by a single, long tone. Then an acknowledgement of eyes opening. Just as quickly as everyone arrived the hall is cleared. I notice there are no sirens as the ambulance leaves. It's anyone's guess right now.

My aide comes to take me to the shower. Life as we know it here goes on.

HALLOWEEN

My very best favorite holiday is Halloween. Yet not this year, I just didn't feel it. LLBFF wanted to decorate my room and I turned her down.

The rec department here has put up decorations on the floor – real honest to God decorations not just some cheap cardboard cutouts.

The therapy department has been discussing costumes for almost my entire stay here. They all dress according to a theme. They chose Peter Pan this year. They told me everyone dresses up. I gave in and the best they would get from me is a T-shirt that says this is my Halloween costume (participation trophy).

Discussions start about the Halloween party. I was opting out after the disaster that was the "special dinner". As the day got closer the party was all the talk. Nope, not going there.

The big day is here. I missed an important part of the equation - the staff parade in their costumes for the residents at the party. ALL OF THE STAFF. The therapists take it one step further and perform a skit and dance. They rock.

Now my afternoon session (which is strategic to coincide with any activity, so I do not have to attend) has to be moved. The therapists will be at the party. Ok, move it up.

Therapy is complete but alas no one is available to take me upstairs. Remember at my age I am not allowed in the elevator unescorted. "Candi, just head over to the party." I am trapped. My PT says come watch our skit. I roll to the party with my rehab mantra going "just kill me now". I move to the back and do not even take a table. If you have a table, you get table mates. The wheelchair locked, away from everyone. Then a table is magically pushed in front of my chair. No thank you I say, please use it for the other residents. Nope. Table it is, and now table mates – "just kill me now".

The entertainer sets up – again karaoke music but he has a guitar. What's next, he puts on a wolfs mask. And sings through the mask while strumming along. Say it with me, "just kill me now".

I start texting friends so they may share in my laudable situation. The gentleman in charge of recreation is thrilled I am here (makes one of us). Can he get me anything? I say look at me, a cold beer would be great if he could hook me up. Dramatic pause. Ok. Be back.

My heart skips a beat. While I had offers of contraband being snuck in, I am still on a handful of meds, so I turned the offers down. But stuck in Halloween hell, screw the meds, it's not like I'm driving. Yellow M&M man tells me he is popping one in the freezer and will be back.

I broke one of my adaptive devices, so I was given a replacement in therapy. If he does not come back with a beer, I will beat him with my adaptation device.

Tables are moved and the entertainment begins. I bring you, the therapists. They were awesome as always. As for the rest of the staff performances, – "just kill me now". No beer, I am getting ready to roll, and then…

The party just got better. Then I got 2 pigs in a blanket and 2 boneless wings (catered from the outside). The food here is so bad that one morning I could not recognize my breakfast. I posted a picture to social media, then called for assistance. I showed them the post, and said I would tag this place if this is not rectified. A number of administrators rush to my room, begging for the picture to be taken down, and next thing I know I have pancakes and juice - without even crying.

When the staff entertainment is done, wolf-man starts to sing. He is not half bad.

Candice, would you like another beer? Yup

I will say the looks I was getting from the other residents who were sipping on their apple juice was comedic. Sorry, no sympathy here. This is my well-earned participation reward. I grab someone on the DL to ask about the beer bounty. There are a few times/events where they allow the residents alcohol (if they are not restricted). There were a few leftover in the back.

I am now a lightweight – 2 beers has become my limit. They laugh and say watch my drinking and driving. I mention that's f'd up to say to someone who is here as a result of a car accident. The looks on their faces seem like they might throw up. Then I burst out laughing. We are all good.

IT'S 3 A.M.

I awoke from a dream. John is coming today. In my dream I got up from my wheelchair and ran across the room to hug him. It was so real – I got up taking a gulp of air but looked down to see my legs in front of me and my adaptive devices on their side of this small bed, always within reach. I have dreamed before of walking but never so real.

This is my dream. dreams come true, just not today. Soon.

I'M A MESS.

John came today. When he walked through the door to my room, I swore my heart stopped. I stood one legged from my chair to grab onto him. When he hugged me all I could think and say was he smelled so good. I forgot how he smells. In five weeks, I forgot how the man that has been part of my life since I'm 15 smelled.

I want him to take a good look at the progress since last he saw me unable to move in this bed. I talk through things I have spoken to him on the phone about, but now he can see in person. I showed him how well my surgical site has healed, but now I know that was a mistake. He sees the scar but remembers the damage. He tries to come back quickly with a joke, but I know. He is jumpy and asks if I am ok or what am I doing at every small move. He does not know my routine. He does not know I am Ironman.

He looks worn and tired. He has been up since 5 am. I try and convince him to nap in my bed to no avail. He does lay down for about 1/2 an hour. We ordered food to be delivered. Having a roommate there is no way to have a halfway normal meal in my room. We go downstairs to the dining/activity room. No one is there past 6, all the residents have to be back on their floors. Not me, this is my new place to escape if I have an escort. I bring my iPad and use the DirectTV app to put on shows we would watch if we were home in our family room.

The food wasn't great, but 5 Star compared to what they serve here. I ordered zeppolis and we spilled powdered sugar and laugh – me more so than him. Then it's time to go back upstairs. My roommate is asleep. We sit for about 5 minutes before his parents come to get him. This is draining us both. They say goodnight and step in the hall to give us some privacy. As I cry into his neck, I tell him again he smells good. My heart is breaking even though we will see each other in the morning. I have 2 therapy sessions tomorrow which I will make sure are back-to-back. I will need to rest after, but then we are going sneaker shopping.

My one good foot is killing me. Now that the therapists continually have me going 100+ feet daily my uninjured leg is screaming. We have had several discussions and I need some new sneakers with a good arch support. I told them I will send John in search of, but the OT who wants me to have my life back says no. Go with him, he says. Get out of here for more than just one scheduled day. John is only here for the weekend, go to the store. He knows I am afraid. He knows I question if I can do it. He knows I need normal.

But how can I be normal right now? My strength has left me as my husband traveled down the road to his folk's home. How can I have normal, and then come back to this - to this place, to this chair, to this bed, to this life? This journey will be long, potentially 2 years, barring the need for an additional surgery. I have no doubt I will make it through whatever I have to do once Home, but that stretch of time between now and then will be my new Everest.

Addendum: I'm not ready to go home. Today was full of lessons I needed to know.

WE WENT SNEAKER SHOPPING

MOST EXPENSIVE PAIR I WILL EVER OWN

We were able to pull right up to the store, easy peasy? Nope. The closest spot was not handicap accessible. Without a placard we could not park in a handicap spot. That meant transferring from the walker to the crutches to get up the curb, then back to the walker.

Explain my situation to a man with the most beautiful eyes in the world. Smart move on the store's part, no one looks at the price. He states they work with many rehab patients and points to a shelf that I should choose from. He measures and measures, considering the swelling and on the 2nd pair we have a winner. My sore foot and leg are smiling. It will take time to get used to them, but the therapists were right. I needed Uber Sneaker. Add in a pair of elastic laces as it will be months before I can tie my shoes and off we go.

We went to John's parents' home. I choose to go with the crutches only.

I am traveling with more things than an infant, walker, crutches, transfer wheelchair, adaptive tools. We had no idea what I will need so we took everything. Guess what? I will need everything.

Driveway to walkway and up 2 small steps then through the door. I decided crutches is the way to go. Until we get on the tile and the crutch slips. Nope, walker it is. See what I mean about lessons learned?

We decide to try and sit in the kitchen. A bit of maneuvering, a pillow added to the chair, and tada - I'm sitting at a kitchen table for the first time in over a month and a half. We have coffee in a real mug. Life is good. John says he will go to White Castle to get lunch. Life got better.

For those who do not know what White Castles are, sorry. It is an acquired taste hamburger that cannot be described. It is the burger of my youth. It screams Home.

He and his dad are gone for quite a while. I am fidgeting. Part of that is not new, it is very difficult to get comfortable, so I always have to shift now. The new twist is I don't know what to do with my hands and arms. My body has now gotten used to sitting in a chair with arms, or holding onto a walker, or crutches, or in a small bed with rails that I constantly have to use to pull myself up. The normalcy of the chair makes me uneasy. There is no safety net. Bobbykins notices and I tell her my dilemma. I then start to pose with my hands and arms in different positions. She laughs and joins in as we "exercise" at the table when John walks back in. More laughter. Yet inside I realize that when the time comes, I will have to relearn normal. It will be uncomfortable going back to my life.

Which brings me to having to pee. Pops ordered a commode to sit over their toilet similar to what I have in rehab. In order to use the rest room, I require handrails. More jokes about they don't need the bucket that came with it but maybe we can use it as a macaroni bowl.

If you have not figured out how big a disruption this is to them, please realize they visit all the time, bring me dinner, clean my clothes, and a host of other things. And in their absolutely stunning home they now have a blue commode so I can come visit for 2 days. Blue, because it's nicer than grey. Unconditional love. More people I can never repay.

John walks next to me like you do with a small child. He does this because we are learning together my limitations outside of my rehab bubble. The powder room is tight, but we figure it out.

We go sit in the tv room. Can I sit on a couch? Yes, with help. Can I get up from the couch? Yes, with a lot of help. Another lesson. I use the recliner and we watch tv – normal. I then started to peruse the eight pounds of medical records from the trauma hospital. I now know much more than I did before. I'll save that for another day. John cat naps. When he wakes up, I need a drink. I have never been so thirsty since starting rehab. Every move expends so much energy.

Next, I try sitting at the dining room table. Tomorrow will be coffee and cake with the family. Another slight success. Let's try another couch. This one is more ass tablet friendly. Regular furniture hurts your ass tablet.

Back to the front room. I fell asleep and wake up in time for dinner – that I could not eat, but I needed more water. I needed a nap so we can get back to rehab and get to bed. Did you get that? I needed a nap so I could get to bed. I am exhausted. And I should pee again before we leave. I have to pre-plan where I will be and when to pee.

Back to rehab with all of my crap. I am not sad for him to go tonight. I am exhausted. I know how long it takes me to get washed and ready for bed. It takes me five minutes to just take off my socks.

I am in bed but fighting to stay up. My meds come at 9 pm. Thank God for daylight savings so I get my extra hour for tomorrow. I text John. I tell him I realize I am not ready to come home, and I need the next few weeks. I admit in a text what I could not say to him – I was devastated when he left last night. I want to go home. Today has given me a list of things to discuss with my therapists so I will truly be ready to go home when the time comes.

DAY PASS #2 A SUCCESS

I will now say an integral part of rehab is knowing your limitations. I am getting better but still struggling. I got picked up a bit earlier today as I had no therapy. Off we went with all my required devices. Considered lessons learned yesterday so today went smoother.

Another normal lunch around the kitchen table. After a bit we moved into the ass tablet friendly living room. John's family started to arrive at different times. Nephews, brothers, and sisters-in-law. A few jokes about how much better I am than the last time they saw me (day of the BOOM). Coffee and cake around the dining room table which was more than filled to capacity. After everyone left, a sharp reminder of why I am still in NY. An episode of pain and increased swelling. To the recliner holding onto John until it passed. I should have remembered my limits and got that side rested earlier. When I awoke from a quick nap the rest of the evening was spent in the travel wheelchair. Two days ago, that may have upset me – that I had no choice but to rely on a chair. That I am not as healed as I thought I was. Tonight, I was grateful we had it. It was a reminder that my healing continues, and I need to remember my limits. Even Ironman cannot go full throttle 24/7. Ironman knows how to play the long game. I'm in it for the long game.

I WAS ASKED TODAY IF IRONMAN HAS A SIDEKICK

I am not a fan of written comic books so for this story I will address the Marvel Universe movies for my answer. Tony Stark aka Ironman went through a transformation beyond just his suit. He started off as a bit of a sanctimonious ass who didn't have anyone close to him. He had people to handle his day-to-day needs, but he was not a relationship guy. Obviously, that changed through the course of his journey. He crumbled and failed on more than one occasion. Yet he was determined to go it alone. He had all of the answers.

He was wrong.

Stark picked up a host of likely and unlikely characters along the way, it takes a village.

Ironman would not be successful if he had a single sidekick (think Batman and Robin). He surrounded himself with people from all walks of life. Yet the most important fact of his crew is that he started to rely on them. As much as he wanted to be able to do everything himself and often felt that the burden of the world rested solely on his shoulders, he accepted help when needed. Let me tell you that is harder than you think. It is humbling, but it also how you gain strength.

As for me, I believed I was the strong one. I was brought to my knees (or more specifically my ass). I had to accept help when every cell in my body was screaming to do otherwise as it was against my nature. I have come to realize that my success will not be diminished by reaching my hand out for assistance. Those on the other side of that hand are not doing so out of pity but do so because they are my sidekicks with a vested interest in my accomplishments. They do so because at the end of the day they want the good guys to win. They are superheroes in their own right. They are the ones who will get me through until I can get home. They are the ones who will continue to fight the good fight by my side.

I remain Ironman now more than ever.

MADE SEVERAL IMPRESSIONS AT REHAB TODAY

I am going to start by saying not everyone believed the impressions to be good.

It was raining on and off today. I didn't wear sweatpants or bring a jacket with me to therapy. There would be no way we would be going outside. Wrong again. "Let's go outside on the crutches" is a sentence someone who cannot walk on their own wants to hear. On a good day, on solid ground, indoors, walking on crutches is a daunting task. Going outside, on wet ground, with leaves all over is just crazy.

Well in real life I will not be able to stay in the safety of my Home because of weather, or if there are things on the ground. Therapy to get me ready for real life. Out we go.

We don't go far, maybe 25 feet, a few turns navigating the leaves and then back in. Ta da! Now what? Crutches slip on wet tile. My awesome new (expensive) sneakers also don't provide great traction on polished tile. Again, now what?

Look around to see what is available to dry the base of the crutches. Don't see anything? Use your socks. This Karate Kid training lets me balance on one foot, take the base of a single crutch, and wipe it on the socks I am wearing. As for sneakers – if there is nothing to dry your feet on baby baby baby steps until you get to safety. I come back into the therapy room and get a towel for my sneakers. A few of my fellow residents ask if I went outside, they were impressed. I am Ironman.

I went back upstairs on the crutches. That's all the way down the hall, in the elevator, and out to the nurse's cart until I needed the chair. My 2nd floor residents and the staff were impressed. Ironman.

Lunch time.

Here is the series of texts I send to friends…

So "lunch" came with only 1 little juice. My aide said the kitchen said I can't have any more juice. I have to call the dietician. Bullshit. I roll myself to the front and tell them get me the dietician. They ask why, and I tell them my juice has been cut off.

I explain that is the best part of the tray and the cups are a mouthful. I need 3 juices. For $9k a week I want my fucking juice back. If I have to call someone outside to bring me juice boxes all hell will be fucking breaking loose here.

I meet with the dietician. A brief basically one-sided conversation ensues. I tell her fix it. She asks my juice preference. Apple in case you are wondering.

They handed me a juice. The aides high five me as they laughed while I rolled back to my room. They were truly impressed.

Apparently, I met my breaking point. It was apple juice. TOTALLY Ironman.

5, 312, 2, 12, ∞

These are significant numbers for today.

5 – after yesterday's debacle I got 5 juices today.

312 – I walked 312 feet outside on crutches. I did not even have a follow with the wheelchair – it stayed behind in my room while I was at therapy.

2 – flights of stairs. I went down one full flight to therapy with one crutch. I then went up one full flight after therapy.

12 – number of days until I am discharged. I will be in rehab 7 weeks and 3 days.

The admissions team came in. They met with my therapists and regardless of what the surgeon says next Friday (weight bearing, no weight bearing, etc.) they said I will be ready to go. I most likely will not be able to return home until the following week as logistically the timing is a nightmare. They are so many things to be coordinated (equipment, doctors, therapy, medicines, durable equipment) as well as trying to get flights with legroom during Thanksgiving. They feel I will be able to do my needed therapy exercises on my own for a week.

Both the therapists pushed me today – to the point I have been in bed for several hours already. Both have discussed aggressive plans with me through next week. Now I understand. They were having a meeting on me this afternoon. Everyone agrees with the plan. I will be home before the end of the month.

The last is the infinity symbol representing the concept of eternity, endless and unlimited. Right now, that is what I feel deep in my heart for the love and support I am blessed to have. The countdown is on.

FULL COURT PRESS

So now that I have been given a discharge day you think I would be coasting in therapy. Nope just the opposite. They have me in a full court press. The weights are heavier, the reps are more, the walking is farther (350 feet today in case you were wondering). I am exhausted.

I am engaging anyone who can hear in my countdown. Will I be with the kids for Thanksgiving is the hot topic everyone wants to know. When I explain it is the unlikeliest scenario, they all jump to Christmas. These residents see milestones – if you don't make one go to the next. There is no time to be wasted on things out of your control. They are cheering me on, they are truly happy that I will soon be on the next phase of my recovery.

I too have become their cheerleader. Yesterday a resident was falling asleep in her wheelchair, she could not even sit up. That happens often, each day presents different problems with their health. I moved my chair closer to hers to make sure she remained safe. Realistically there was little I could do if she slipped out of her chair or fell forward. However, I could touch her shoulder, so she knew she was not alone. I could alert a therapist when her foot slipped between the supports. She is part of my crew. Today was a better day for her, her son was here, and we all clapped and yelled as she performed one of the exercises that mimics a child's game.

Then the 4th floor resident who "works" in the therapy room came down. She and I sit near each other most afternoons as I finish the latter part of my second session. We chat that I am now a short timer. There are a number of residents whose full stay is less than the time I have left, but for a 4th floor – they are never going back home.

She stops what she is doing, looks me in the eye, and says she will miss me. In that moment I realize I will miss her as well. Tomorrow she will bring her phone down and I will program my number. I tell her I will write; I know how much the notes and cards I received cheered me up on the dark days. She responds she cannot longer write like she used to, her hands are careworn and often betray her.

I will write. I will call.

The therapist has me go back up the steps to my room. I am dog tired. As I rest on the landing, we talk about the things people take for granted. Before I know it, what is in my heart is pouring out of my mouth. This injury has forever changed me. I will never take the little things for granted again. I will never be able to forget the people who changed my life here. She states she feels the same – doing what she does, seeing what she sees has changed her also.

Then I finish the stairs. That's what we do. We keep moving on.

LAUGHTER THROUGH THE PAIN

In the middle of the night, I felt like someone had stabbed me by the groin. As I woke up in bed alone that was not the case. It was difficult and painful to get out of bed (more so than usual). This happened several times through the night. This is in addition to being cooked as the heat is sooooo high to keep the elderly residents warm. Opening the windows, the few inches I can (else there are some days I might jump) brought no relief as there was no breeze. I tried and was successful to get the small fan on the wall working. When all else failed I beat it with my crutch.

I thought maybe a hot shower might help, but no. But today I was able to dress myself with no help in the shower room. Another milestone. If only they would let me take a shower on my own. Who am I kidding, I can't ride the elevator without a chaperone.

No rest for the wicked at therapy. When the therapist came to my room this morning, I stated the discomfort and issues I was having. Standard answers of I am doing more, swelling will happen, pain is to be expected for quite some time, weather may be playing a factor. Oh, and go ahead and walk downstairs to therapy.

I will have to say practicing stairs is the craziest and hardest thing they have me do. When I ask why this torture, the PT states what if I am going somewhere and the elevator doesn't work? I told her I will tell them to come down, or I will come back later. In order to do stairs you have to hold both crutches in one hand using them as a crutch, while using the other to hold onto the banister and pull yourself with every ounce of strength while you hop to the next stair on one foot. You keep doing that until you are up (or down) the stairs or die trying.

Session one in the books, but now I have to walk back to my room. The therapists will not allow me to take my wheelchair any longer as they are pushing me my last week+. I am as always exhausted and all I want to do is get back to bed. But now I start to think, when will I have to pee? Is the pain of getting out of that bed worth not wetting the bed? That's how I knew it was a really bad day – when I was contemplating peeing the bed. I shake it off and my mom genes kick in. I always told the kids go do your last 2 drops before we had to go anywhere. The standard answer? I don't have to go. The mom response? Just go sit on the toilet. I would always hear them pee. So, toilet sitting it is. For the record it works I did pee.

Into bed which also was a task. My right leg is uncooperative today, so I had to strap my foot and literally pull it into bed. And everything hurt. As I try and catch my breath a staff member brings me a package. Great, these should be my replacement headphones. Nope. Furthest thing. I got a horse's head mask. A friend from work who has been one of my staunchest cheerleaders and continues to bring normal into my far from normal life understands that Don Puleo needs to send a message. No one will ever f' with my juice again.

I laugh – a belly laugh that hurts my ass tablet even more. I cannot stop. I know this present deserves a place here, but not sure where that will be. As I wasn't getting up just yet, I place the head on top of the crutches which are held by Velcro to my bed. Every time I turn, I laugh as it looks at me. Aides come in to do their cursory check and jump back when they see the head. Which makes me laugh. They don't get the reference.

Much to my surprise not everyone has seen the Godfather. I think that may be part of the reason the country is in such disarray. All of the answers to life's tough issues are in The Godfather.

- Leave the gun, take the cannoli.

- Monday Tuesday Thursday.

- It's not personal, it's business.

- Don't ever take sides against the family.

- I'm going to make him an offer he can't refuse.

The list goes on.

No one here gets the horse head reference. After asking again if they saw the movie I give up and say it's a joke gift to make me laugh. The only one I take the time to explain it to is the afternoon therapist. I'm sending a message about my juice.

The afternoon session starts like the morning one – walk down the stairs. I hate these stairs. I am tired of lugging both crutches. I just want to throw the crutch up to the landing and hope for the best. At the end of the session even heat did not release the pain. As she pokes and prods, she believes it is a muscle contraction that won't release. No position works for her to release it. I would need to get on my belly for her to try again but I can't do that. The hope is tomorrow will be a better day as I hobble back.

LLBFF comes over and we laugh about the gift. I am in bed yet again. I was going to get out, but I know she understands. We will make small talk with me in bed and she in my wheelchair. I state he needs a name. "Apple" comes out of her mouth without hesitation. Next thing we start making videos on my phone.

This was just the beginning. Apple will most likely end up with a YouTube channel. A series of pictures and more stupid videos ensue. And we laugh and laugh some more. I can't help but text the lovely lady who sent this. I text she has no idea how much I needed this today. She didn't know about the pain. She didn't know about today's struggles. She only knew I needed a laugh.

When the BOOM happened, I looked on the internet for someone in my situation so I could see what my life was going to be like, looking for a day-to-day guide, but I found nothing. My wish in writing this is my story fills that void for someone. I purposefully do not name those who helped me. Yet I cannot thank them enough. When I started this I didn't know where it would end up. As such I was careful with references, my family and LLBFF aside as this is their journey too. The stronger I get the more I want to put peoples name up in neon lights.

As LLBFF gets ready to leave I check on my roommate. She had asked for a pain killer, and I don't think she got it. I roll to the front and bring this to someone's attention as I stay in the hall. LLBFF stays too, she wants to see how this ends up. Someone gets on it right away. Is it because I have been a vocal resident? Because she is related to a staff member? Or is Apple already hard at work?

I HAD A GREAT CHILDHOOD

I believe every parent wants better for their children. I know John and I certainly do. The world has changed so much since we were kids. My mother would not think twice about giving me thirty-five cents to get on a bus from the Bronx to Queens to see my sister (with a transfer in between). We knew to be home by the time the streetlights were on. Every Halloween a neighbor would make homemade candy apples and tell us to let our parents know who they were from. We sat on stoops, listened to music on BOOM boxes and played stickball in the streets. We relished our friends and were fiercely loyal. We didn't have a ton of money, but it didn't matter. My best memories of my youth involved my circle of friends.

Then life got in the way. We grew up and, in some cases, grew apart. I can honestly say time and distance does not diminish my memories. These feelings I still hold in my heart are what I wished for my children, but their childhood was different. Changes in society made us more protective, even today we make sure our sons have their cell phones with them in case of emergency. They grew up with organized activities, they needed to tell us where they were going and who they would be with. None of the yelling "going out" that we used to do. My heart would skip a beat when they left the house. Are they safe? Will the world be kind? Every bad thing in the news now became something that could happen to my children.

Are things really that much worse? Or do we just know more now? Did the media influence the way we raised our children? I felt my children were protected and not as savvy as we were growing up. I share part of the blame. I've had a lot of loss in my lifetime and the very thought of something happening to my sons is paralyzing.

These children who grew up in the digital age, the age of social media and video games have a different view on life. They sit at a table and text the person sitting next to them. They play online games with their friends instead of engaging. The way they interact is so vastly different than we did. The way they treat relationships sometimes boggles my mind.

Yet it is through social media that I found people again. My childhood and high school friends. People who had moved away and contact was lost for years. How wonderful what a few searches can yield. I have come to know them again, this time as adults instead of the youths in my memories. I see their children, and children's children. Successes are celebrated, losses are mourned. Sometimes a chuckle is all that is shared.

I am still wondering why this "BOOM" happened. I may never know the reason. I could state unequivocally if this happened 15 years ago, I would be lost. But social media and texts and emails and cell phone calls and FaceTime has not only let me communicate with my loved ones far away but brought people back into my life. Perhaps that was meant to be. I had equated the death of a classmate with a pebble cast unto the water. The effects of the ripples felt by her passing was felt far and wide. I am seeing that again with my recovery. I am touched by the outpouring of good wishes, but also see that where I am now – that I will persevere – that strength comes from within, has affected others as well.

This BOOM led me to multiple visits today. Two childhood friends that I have not seen in what feels like a lifetime. Yet it felt like no time had passed. I want them to know the visit warmed my heart. But I will say the hugs warmed my soul. Real hugs.

I have previously referenced another longtime friend that visits regularly. But the more I thought about her tonight, she is my family too. Her visits bring normal into my life more than I can ever express.

Family members came by, as always with love and warmth (and food).

What I was able to experience today some people will never know in a lifetime. So even though there is still pain and discomfort, today was a great day that I am thankful for. I will go to bed tonight knowing I am loved. Tomorrow will be a new day, and one day closer to that first step.

I BROKE MY STREAK

I was on a 32-day streak for updating my journal. It has and most likely will continue to be what keeps me sane. It is my therapy without a therapist for now. Yet yesterday I skipped updating. The last several days have been overwhelming both physically and emotionally. It took a little bit to be able to process.

When I was 14 my father died. He was hospitalized but I did not know until his last few days how serious it was. My mother, right or wrong, made the decision to not tell me. She felt there would be no good to come of knowing before his time as it would not change the outcome. At the time I was angry. I told her I would have done some things differently. Today, as I sit in a wheelchair, I did the same to my children. I understand now.

There are a handful of very vivid memories surrounding his death, memories that I continue to see as a snapshot of time. One of them was when I came into the church for his funeral mass and saw a sea of blue. My classmates, my SCA sisters, showed up in full force. They were there to offer their prayers and to let me know I was not alone. There was strength in their numbers. I don't know if they saw me cry when I looked at them. I don't know if they thought it was the tears I was shedding all day as there were a lot of them. I don't think I ever told them what them having there meant. There was an incident which took several years before it resolved that overshadowed the rest of the day. I was young and I was angry, and I was wrong. It took about 3 years before I was able to say that and to make amends. I should have thanked them and told them then how they helped me.

Yesterday afternoon began with a visit from some of these ladies. Several schoolmates and one of our favorite teachers (not starting a war here) came from the Tri-State area to spend some time. It was best summed up as **"#wehadasmallfeast"**. Pizza and delicacies and cookies and pastries and a smuggled bottle of wine. I sat at the table in my chair with my bad leg raised. They didn't care. They were not there for my injury; they were there for me.

***BTW there was apple juice. ***

Just like the day before, time and distance faded immediately. Like those many years ago, they were there to support me and let me know I am not alone. This time I want them all to know what having their support at another low point in my life means to me – I am humbled, and I am blessed, and I am thankful. These ladies, every single one of them, has had extreme loss and difficulties at some point in their lives. Yet they emerged stronger. I take that as a sign that this too shall pass. We took a picture to commemorate the visit.

Later in the day my niece came by to introduce me to her serious boyfriend. Not the way I ordinarily would like to meet new people, but I am going with the flow. I needed to stay on the bed and again my injury and the circumstances was ignored.

PS – I like him.

This weekend was more than just having company and catching up with old friends. This weekend was also a next step for me. I have been in a cocoon of hospitals and rehab for almost 2 months now. While I look a hell of a lot better than when this started there are undisputed facts; the swelling in my lower extremities especially the operative side is crazy again, I am in a wheelchair, I can't walk without crutches or a walker and then for at most 350 feet, pain is part of my day to day. This is my new normal and will be for quite some time.

But I have to start living again. I have to start having interactions that do not rely solely on technology.

I have to get ready to face my children. Read this sentence again please.

I have to get ready to face my children.

I have to get used to the look on people's faces when they see me in this chair. I have to learn true love and friendship comes without pity. I have to learn to take the badass Ironman that lives here and make sure she is just as strong in the real world. I have so, so much to learn.

These people from my past, that I equate with happiness and love and support and wonderful memories are the people I chose to walk with me on this next step.

For those I have not seen, I wish to thank you again. The cards, the texts, the funny gifs sent via Instant Messenger – I cherish each one. You don't know how sometimes when I return from a tough therapy session or awake with a middle of the night cramp how these put a smile on my face. I am often too tired to respond, so please know the strength you give me in my journey.

DANCE PARTY

Technically my last therapy sessions will be this Saturday, but they will not be with my regular therapists. Friday will be my dance party. I am torn. This is the day in rehab. This dance deems me ready to go (yay!!!!), but also ends this part of my journey with the people I will forever credit with giving me back my life (boo hoo).

The last time I deliberated so much over a song choice was my wedding. This choice, like that one, will bring me back to a pivotal time in my life every time I hear it. It needs to be epic. It needs to be Ironman worthy.

Right now, I am leaning towards Amy Winehouse's Rehab. It has all of the components, great beat, something you can dance to, and come on – the lyrics are killer ...

"They tried to make me go to rehab. I said, no, no, no"

I am putting it out there. Offer up suggestions. Keep in mind when I say this is my dance party, I can only stand on one leg and if I move around a bit, I need to hold on to something else I will re-break my ass tablet. Think "dance" like the little kids on Wonderama.

Text, instant message, carrier pigeon, respond anyway you can. Get your vote out. Winner will be announced Thursday.

DANCE PARTY UPDATE

The responses so far have been amazing. Been listening to music all morning. I would like to offer some honorable mentions for making me laugh, but are not in the current top 10:

- Safety dance

- Back on my feet again

- I'm still standing

I am on the fence on where Titanium should be placed. Decided to use it to round off the current top of the charts.

- On top of the world: Imagine Dragons

- Rehab: Amy Winehouse

- Roar: Katy Perry

- Stronger: Kelly Clarkson

- Champion: Carrie Underwood

- The Climb: Miley Cyrus

- The Comeback: Danny Gokey

- Rise Up: Andrea Day

- Titanium: Sia

Surprisingly I am now changing my vote and leaning towards Champion.

Keep 'em coming

DREAMS

I am not sure if I dream more now than before the BOOM. The longer I am away from home the more I seem to have difficulty remembering small things like that. My life seems to be separated; before 9/19 and after. I think that will forever be the case. I can only hope that there will be many happy tick marks on the timeline of my life that will move the BOOM farther away.

I have dreams of my family, of working, of sitting on my patio with the dog, and of course of walking. Last night I awoke with a start because I believed I was sleeping on my side. Of course, when I looked down my legs were stretched out right in front of me. But it felt so real. I began to think maybe I did roll over in my sleep. This kept me up for several hours.

Finally, I couldn't take it anymore, I had to know. I placed a pillow between my legs, not an easy task, and tried to roll to my side. The PT said it was safe to be on my side if I stabilized my legs with a pillow. However, when we tried it together it was too much for me, so we abandoned that exercise.

I moved maybe 2 inches. I held onto the side rails of the bed to anchor me and pull a bit more. I gave up as I didn't want to hurt myself. Almost 2 months and I can't roll onto my side unassisted.

In my pre 9/19 life I slept in every position except the one I am regulated now. What I would give to be able to roll on my stomach, grab a pillow with both arms and sleep. It seems for now I will only do so in my dreams.

TAKING STOCK

Brief Power outages are something I am getting used to here. It seems to happen several times a week. Yesterday there was a loud BOOM, then the power went out. The backup generator kicked on, but not everything was working. The PT came to get me and said we have to do the stairs as the elevators are offline. I asked her before we went are the stair locks working because there is no way I was going to be stuck on the stairway. She said we were good.

There is no security here. Someone directs you in the lobby, most times. Anyone can get in here at anytime. Like the elevators on the upper floors, the stairs have an electronic pass lock. This prevents the wandering patients from being able to escape.

PT went much better than the day before. The muscle relaxers I am now taking stops the screaming pain in my groin. I have actually been able to sleep up to 4 hours now. I look around and a number of patients are just sitting there. They explain the elevators are still not working so they can't go up, and new patients can't come down.

Finally, one of the PTs goes to a closet and pulls out a guitar. She plays and starts to sing. There is now a sing a long going on. She could have easily sat there playing on her phone, yet she did something to engage the patients. Again, this is the difference of the rehab staff vs. the care staff.

The rehab staff cares. Rehab plus 5.

I was able to walk back up to my room (sounds so casually easy – walk up to my room. It's not). They get 1 elevator working and start to get the residents back to their rooms ASAP. TV is out and patient rooms on the other side of the hall are dark. My room is ok. We are only 1 of 3 rooms that have lights in our bathroom on this floor.

TV and music are the biggest part of the resident's life. Imagine how they are without it. I say a thank you prayer to Steve Jobs for my iPad.

My dear friend brings pizza and the Con Ed trucks continue to look for the problem. This started at 2 pm. Trucks come and go. By 9 pm they are all gone and don't come back. My roommate's daughter brings us LED lanterns just in case. This morning no progress is made. More CNAs are here today than I have ever seen, but the care is worse. They blame the power loss, but the partial power and the generators are doing their job. Rehab vs. care staff – care staff is now 5 to minus 3.

My roommate, while very articulate, has her routine. As there is no tv she decides she will recite the tv schedule for me. This way I will know what we are missing. ***sigh***

I am trying to get a shower. They say they will check and get back to me. Nobody comes back. I roll myself to the shower room – there is light. I go to the nurse's station to ask about a shower. They tell me lights are out. Nay nay I say. I saw it with my own 2 eyes. They will tell the aide.

The aide stops in. Shower? Lights but they don't think there is hot water. They will check. No one comes back.

Roommate's daughter checks, there is hot water. However, it is now breakfast time so there is no one to take me. ***sigh*** care staff -6

I get dressed and decide to start going through the things I have accumulated. I make separate piles; keep here for now, send with the parents, give to 4th floor residents. The last pile is the biggest. It is through the generosity of people who love me I am able to pay it forward. The only issue is how to get this booty safely upstairs, so it does not fall into the wrong hands. When everything is back online, they will escort me.

Breakfast is also late. Par for the course. The therapy assistant pops in to say we will be doing therapy in the day room. Crutches only as there is no room for the chair. Off I go.

Then usually morose day room has come to life. Patients are squeezed into every nook and cranny along with the residents who do not have any lights. PTs run up and down the stairs to get what they need. They are also working in the hallway and in patient's rooms. Whatever it takes to get the job done. Rehab +7

As I sit by the doorway doing my strength training, I am eavesdropping on a conversation of several aides. One in part is very vocal about how she does not believe management treats her fairly. Like docking her pay when she is late. I shake my head. She then goes on to state things I already know because I experienced them firsthand. How she pushes patients to the next shift when she does not feel like dealing with the issue. How she makes patients wait for things because she feels there is no rush. The culmination of her bullshit comes when a PT goes to the water container they use for the day room. She grabs the PTs arm and says don't drink that. When asked why she replied back is this for you? When the PT says no, it for a patient, she says then ok. But don't you drink from that, only them. There is other water for the staff. Minus 20.

One of the reasons I hoard my juice is so I have something to drink at night. I don't trust the aides to fill my water container. There are aides I will not even let make my bed. My half ass tablet bed making is better than letting some of them do it.

My MFA is here today but not assigned to me. Yet she sneaks me a quick shower while everyone else is in the day room. Plus 5 for her alone.

I make my bed and get back in it. I am trying to reduce the swelling as much as possible. This is already a long day.

IT'S NOT ANYTHING YOU DID

There was no dance party today. We entered our 3rd day of electric/power problems that was exasperated by a snowstorm. Therapy was moved to the day (of the dead) room with patients that had no lights in theirs. One of the supervisors came to tell me all doctors appointments were being canceled due to horrible road conditions. I needed to see the surgeon, I wanted to, or thought I did, know how I am. I was upset but went to therapy. They were trying to reschedule, I said I needed to be seen ASAP else I would go today, AMA. I need to go home.

Pops texts me to say he was out, and the roads were clear. Off to investigate. Sure enough, he is right. Appointments were canceled because the elevators are broke. Both of them. This is more than power problems. I have been doing stairs for 2 weeks- I tell them make sure they get the appointment back. They tell me it's not safe. Let's just say I got my appointment back – a PT just has to do the stairs with me.

Off to the doctor. I have my Ironman shirt on. I've got this. X-rays less painful than last time. BS stuff with the nurse and we wait. And wait. And wait. New nurse comes in and puts the X-rays up and leaves. We look – they look just like the last ones.

The Dr. comes in sad faced and asked how am I doing? Discuss general ass tablet things and tell him I am getting pain in my groin, and I feel some movement in the hip. I expect to hear what I have been hearing – to be expected, it will lessen, its musculature. Nope, he points to the X-ray and brings up the old one to compare. We don't see the difference until he points to it. A small section of bone shifted. He looks at me and says,

It's not anything you did.

I know that's no good. The bone died. The trauma was just too much. He talks through the surgical plan he did, shows me pre-op scans, and more. He is justifying his surgery. I cry. Part of me wants to say look at all of the pieces you had to put together; you did a great job. That part of me is not speaking. Practical me wants to know what's next. Can I fly home?

Yes, I am now cleared to fly. Will be a few weeks. I can start weight on my leg. Increments over the next month. Hip restrictions are lifted.

There will be pain. There will be things I will try and find too difficult because of the pain. Walking will be painful. I may get to the point where I only need 1 crutch. Yes, keep the wheelchair. I should get full use of my leg eventually.

Someday the pain will be more than I can bear. When that happens, I will need to have the full replacement surgery I wanted in the first place, but was in no condition to get. I have to keep to the original plan and push myself to be able to walk. However, I now know that will include pain. Increasing pain. With dead broken bones. How do you make yourself work toward that goal?

Today I am broken again. I have nowhere to go where I can be by myself and have the breakdown I think I need. We stop back at the house, so I do not have to face the rehab center after the bad news. I cry. I call John. He is broken too. Back to rehab. The PT is expecting good news – I have none. The elevators are still out so we walk up the stairs. I say goodbye to Pops. He has been there through this entire ordeal. I just can't be around him tonight. I cannot have my pain be his. I text my friends – I love them but can't talk to them either. I wonder what my dreams will be.

WHAT DID HE LOSE?

I have a raging headache. The tears and the anger are my undoing. Today I do not even want to be out of this hospital bed. I want to roll over on my side and pull the covers over my head and sleep the day away. I do not remember ever wanting to drink and be numb more than right now.

I don't have that luxury. Like clockwork the nurse comes in and wakes me for early morning medication. I can't roll on my side, and I have 2 therapy sessions today. The fucking bed alarms from patients getting up who should not be blaring. I leave the curtain up between me and my roommate. She can look out the other window today. She will be fine. I am still having a breakdown.

I hate this shit hole of a place. I want to leave today.

The hope that has kept me pushing is gone. I would do anything, be anywhere, withstand all of the crap once I thought I would have my life back eventually. I knew the journey would be long and rough and I was ready to tackle it. Without hope I cannot face what is still ahead of me.

Initially I was resigned to the fact that I may be in a wheelchair. But when I "walked", when I had a glimpse of what was possible, I was determined. I don't have that anymore. It's like a gift was ripped from my arms. It is a loss I was not ready for.

What did the other driver lose? His car? Which is more than likely already replaced. Does he have the nightmares I do? Did he lose precious time with his family? Did he lose any dignity by having to rely on strangers for even the most basic functions? Did he fucking walk into his shower today? I could keep going. Will his life be measured by pain? Is his family suffering because of his carelessness? When did he get his life back?

I am angry.

I am hurt.

I am broken.

I don't need pep talks. I don't need to be told I am strong, and I can do this. I don't need reminders that I am lucky to be alive. For now, I need to be fucking angry.

PICKING UP THE PIECES

My wheelchair got delivered today. Directly to my room along with the other tools I need to lead my life. Of course, the order was wrong. I could not get anyone to respond to the call bell, so the delivery guy left. When finally, someone came in, I asked for the social worker. They don't work weekends. I explained that after having 3 meetings reviewing what was needed, the order was wrong. No one to help until Monday.

I ask how I am getting out of here with a chair and all my crap with no elevators. Dramatic pause.

They don't know.

I have been bequeathing my things to those I leave behind. But I wanted to say goodbye in person to my 4th floor friend. It does not look like that will happen as she is being held hostage by the lack of elevators. I can't do 2 flights up and down just yet.

The OT asks how things are. He makes me cry just by the look on his face. I apologize and say I'm broken.

He stays with me until I am better. I show him my PT script for when I go home and ask him to review it with me so I understand. Off to the day (of the dead) room again for therapy. He makes slight changes to our routine. He is getting me ready to work on my own. These are things that need to stay as part of my daily routine to keep up my strength. He reminds me when I got here, I was in bad shape because of the BOOM. By the time the need for a 2nd surgery comes around I will start off strong. The next recovery will not be the same as this. In the meantime, I can work around the pain.

The PT mirrors the sentiment. She described in detail rehabilitation for the eventual 2nd surgery. Just keep working, don't stop, and I will be fine. She works with me on my new weight bearing therapy.

They don't coddle me.

They say these things not to cheer me up, but so I know what my personal responsibilities need to be to live my life and prepare for whatever comes next.

I come back and rest. I talk with John. He and I are unsure of how to deal with the news. We talk of calls we have to make and as always that we love each other. He is trying to find me a way home. I have to deal with my treatment plan when I get back. We hang up with promises to talk later. I then fall asleep, and when I awake my LLBFF is here. I think the smell of the fries is what wakes me. We have a moment. Actually, we have several. She is the bringer of greasy food, ice cream and beer. She knows me. She is still my cheerleader but knows not to go overboard today.

I ask her to make the trip to the 4th floor to bring my friend what I have put aside for her. She navigates her way to bring gifts to this stranger. This resident who thrives on social interactions has been sidelined because of the power/elevator situation. Of course, she engages in a conversation. She asks if we are sisters. She gives LLBFF her contact info. I will write to her. I understand how correspondence can brighten your day.

My children have called her Aunt LLBFF their entire lives. They never met my father. A few years ago, LLBFF's dad had some health issues. The boys heard me talking to John and questioned me. How could her dad have a problem? My kids grew up thinking we were sisters, that we had the same father. We get that often.

Fast forward and I get a visitor. Another resident's daughter. We have bonded over this place. Mostly how bad it is to be here. It is not what she wants for her mom, but the therapists are the best. She knows I am leaving soon so she came to say goodbye. She asks if LLBFF and I are sisters. Told you this happens a lot.

She then shares issues in her life. Her story and mine both suck. She needs to vent, and she knows this is a safe place. LLBFF can't believe how much and the quick pace of her sharing with virtual strangers. I understand. I think it's easier to tell a stranger than someone you care about. Again, you don't want to make your pain their pain. I give her my contact info.

I have no choice but to rise up to the new challenges set before me. Giving up is not an option. I am still angry, but a hug from my LLBFF goes pretty far. As does cold beer.

MY LAST THERAPY SESSIONS – I DID NOT FINISH

Day 5 of power/elevator issues. Day of the dead room for therapy. The power issues are wreaking havoc. Everything is being shuffled up and down the stairs. Every meal is late. The staff is for the most part pitching in to cover as best they can. But they, along with the residents, have had it. The have none of the interaction they are used to. The food service which is generally bad is worse. One resident got a moldy piece of bread. The maintenance guy is running extension cords. At least the heat is on, else these elderly patients would be in peril.

Mostly everyone knows by now that I am leaving tomorrow, and that the surgery was not as successful as we had hoped. I have spoken to more people today than through all my time here. They have been cheering me from the sidelines and offer encouragement. They are happy I am getting out of here. There is sadness in their eyes because they are staying in this mess.

Before the Dr. appt I had started to give away my things, very similar to when you leave jail. I stopped when I got the news I did not want to hear. Today I rolled around the floor and handed out Frappuccinos, juice, and candy. I said my goodbyes. As bad as I feel right now these people need a break. I keep the skeleton and the horse's head.

I'll be fine.

I really believe that now. I needed that breakdown that was building. I imagine that will happen from time to time. I am sure it will happen on days when the pain is too much.

The therapists were trying to conduct the sessions with me. But they too were trying to help the residents for whom they truly care about. I needed to do some of the weight bearing exercises to learn what to do when on my own and how to apply it when walking with the crutches. It is different. It is uncomfortable. Muscles that have only been manually manipulated are being put back to work. It is odd to see my foot on the ground. I can tell exactly where the shifted bone is now. Certain movements make it grind. I will try not to move that way.

When I have learned all I need, I bow out of the remaining time. I am sweaty and tired. The last few emotional days have taken their toll. I just want a shower. The therapists tell me my main PT wants to see me before I leave tomorrow. I owe her a dance.

I tell my most favorite aide who is helping me shower how much I appreciate everything she did for me while I was here. I don't think she gets many thank you's.

I will be going out today for Bobbykin's lasagna. They tell me I can't leave. It's not safe. I tell them bite me. I go to the supervisor on shift who does not know me. He fills in occasionally on the weekends. I tell him I am going out. I am taking the stairs. He seems unsure. I tell him I'm going. We compromise by having a PT say I am good to go. I tell him they cannot keep me as a prisoner.

John lets me know he was able to get us a flight home. It will be 12/2. There are no available seats with the legroom I require until then due to the holiday. He states the airline was very helpful on the phone. He was instructed on how we are to travel with the wheelchair. He will be flying in on our wedding anniversary. For that I am grateful. We have a lot to celebrate.

I will be fine.

I'M TO BE DISCHARGED TODAY

Yet we are in day 6 of power issues. They do not believe the generator has enough voltage to power the elevator without tripping the circuit. The new generator is supposed to come today.

If they think I am waiting for a potential delivery and installation of a generator they are out of their fucking minds.

The other option is for them to get help to get me, my wheelchair, and all of my clothes, blanket, and misc. stuff down the stairs.

Stay tuned.

FREEDOM!

I am out of rehab and in the in law halfway house for 2 weeks until I can get a flight home.

I was ready to go by 7 a.m.

The parade of useless people started at 9. Had to review again the incorrect equipment/tools. Discharge will be at 11.

Can I go down the stairs? How many times have we had this discussion since last week? They are now sure there is not enough power to run the elevators without them tripping the circuit and getting trapped. I would have hated to be the test subject for that. I tell them Pops is not hauling all my stuff downstairs. They will get us people.

So, I wait.

My OT comes into my room. We had already said goodbye on Saturday. He wanted to see me again. He wanted to talk and encourage me to finish strong. Don't let the eventual second surgery get me down. We talk again about the condition I was in when I got here, how broken the BOOM left me. How I could not even move in the bed. Look, he said, really look at what I have achieved. Anything after this will be a piece of cake. We talk a bit more. He makes me cry. We hug goodbye and I thank him again. A bitchy nurse comes by to see if I want my morning meds. She tells the OT I will not cry for her. **#truth**

A young nurse I befriended is not working my floor today. She makes a point to come by to give me a hug and say I remain in her prayers. She will miss me. I tell her too that her family is in my prayers. They are dealing with a loved one with end stage cancer. We had many chats during my stay. She

71

deserves better than here. I hope she realizes that one day. Her compassion for her patients is lost on this administration.

The therapy assistant pops in to wish me well. A number of others stop by to say their goodbyes. My roommate wants a hug and a kiss. She will be leaving this week as her daughter worries that I will not be there to keep an eye on things.

The housecleaner wants to clean the room. She is still a little pissed since I put the horse head in my bed and went to therapy. She asks if I am going home, I nod yes. She stops and smiles and pats me on the shoulder. You are just fine, she says. She too wishes me well. I guess we are friends again.

I roll into the hall to let her do her thing. From down the hall I hear my name. It is my PT. WE DID NOT DANCE she exclaims! It's ok I say as I hug her goodbye and through some tears thank her for giving me back some independence, for literally getting me back on my feet for however long, for giving me hope.

No. She is not leaving. She walks on the just washed floor to get my crutches. Pointing to my iPad she says YouTube the song. She says it's not the dance party I should have gotten but we are going to dance it out. So this bundle of joy has me dancing to Amy Winehouse in the hallway on a pair of crutches. We laugh, we cry, we hug. I don't think she will ever know how she changed my life. She places her hands on my shoulders and looks me in the eye. Keep in touch. I will.

Pops gets here. True to their word this time, the maintenance guy helps him haul my crap. I work on getting my prescriptions straightened out. That too is a mess. No surprise. Therapy patients and residents seeking light cram the halls and the day room. Alarms are blaring every few minutes, either from residents getting up from their beds or people opening the doors to the stairwell. They now have a sign at the nurse's station that they are working with ConEd on the power. Bullshit.

We finally leave.

IT'S 2:17 AM

Don't get me wrong, I am thrilled to be out of rehab. But it is hard getting used to life on the outside.

The bars on the bed which confined me are not here to help me pull myself up and out. The couch I use does not let me control the height to be able to put my shoes on without the pain of trying to raise my leg. Every chair here is not higher, wider and have strong arms to let me sit and stand easily. The powder room cannot accommodate my wheelchair when I am too tired to use the crutches or a walker.

It's rough getting used to real life when I am still broken.

While I enjoy sitting at the table to eat meals out of my chair, it is difficult to maneuver. Doing my first day of PT on my own included knocking around on my crutches in a home vs. the expanse of the halls. My super heating pad buy from Amazon pales in comparison to the heat generated from the moist heat pads of rehab.

However, I slept soundly and longer with fewer times up last night than I have in the last 2 months. It was wonderful not to be woken up at midnight and five in the morning by nurses, or have a roommate turn on the lights in the room when calling for an aide. I hope to catch up on missed sleep during my stay.

It's past 2 am and I can't get settled back to bed. I could use a drink but am weighing how tired I am to go to the kitchen and get some water. The benefit of being in that hospital setting was everything was close to hand.

Everything took longer today. Longer to go to the bathroom, longer to get dressed, longer to cleanup my temporary bed/couch. Tonight, like last night, I am dividing my time between sleeping stretched out on the couch vs. using the recliner. My ass tablet can't decide how to get comfortable.

But I did make my own breakfast today. It was only cereal but I navigated to get milk, the cereal, a bowl and spoon onto the table. I could have used a nap afterwards. These small mundane tasks are still robbing my energy.

I am learning how to live again. Then I will do it again when I get to my home. Then I will do it again when I return to work. Then I will do it again and again and again each time I am in a new environment.

But I am living again.

THANKSGIVING

I am torn this Thanksgiving.

- I miss my husband and children.

- I was able to speak with them today and hear the banter that fills our home. I heard the love.

- I want to be home.

- I had a wonderful thanksgiving with family. This home too is filled with love.

- I had to take a painkiller.

- I am alive.

OFF TIME

I haven't updated my journal in several days.

I am going to repeat something I wrote several days ago…

It's rough getting used to real life when I am still broken.

I read through the notes prepared by the surgeon for the doctor who will be taking over my care in Florida. I look at the shots to prevent blood clots I will need to self-administer when it becomes time to fly. I continue with my PT exercises, not wanting to lose any ground I worked so hard for. I sweat through the weights. I am forging ahead, or so I think.

It's been cold and rainy these last few days. This home is warm and inviting, but my injury seems to know the weather.

The pain has been unrelenting. The painkillers and muscle relaxers are not helping. I can't get comfortable. It hurts every time I have to get up. I miss my family. I need to be home. I feel like my halfway house stay is proving that I am failing.

Sleep eludes me. One night I do not go to sleep until 6:30 a.m. That's right 6:30 a.m.

Then I take a day off. I can't. I just can't. There is a correlation between the level of my pain and my strength to keep on.

Today warms up and the sun peeks out. Even though I have not left the house, my injury again knows. The swelling while ever present is not as bad. The pain is not as bad. Back to full PT exercises.

I can only assume this will be my life, outside influences affecting my day to day. Tomorrow I will be sending my job a list of accommodations I need in order to eventually get back to the office. A chair not on wheels with arms so I can lift myself up. The ability to accommodate my wheelchair if needed, my crutches. In my mind I am estimating the steps from the door to the elevators, from my office to the ladies' room, to the conference rooms. I begin to think that I won't be getting any food from the cafe – there is no way to carry food with my crutches. I am thinking I need an industrial grabber for work to be able to access my files. I bought a backpack so I can take notepads and such to meetings.

I am forging ahead. I have to plan 50 steps ahead when I literally can take none.

I'LL BE RIGHT BACK; I JUST HAVE TO PEE REAL QUICK...

That phrase never comes out on my mouth these days. Having several bad days put me back in super planning mode. It hurts to get up, so I plot and plan every move. If I have to pee, I now spend extra time sitting on the toilet just in case I can go more. The thought of having to get up again in less than several hours saddens me.

I used the wheelchair more today than in recent days. I have realized that too will be something I need to plan for. You know what? That's ok. Using the wheelchair means I'm mobile. There will be good days, there will be bad days. I have to learn to plan for both.

I am counting down until I see John again, until I can go home, until I see my boys. Even Cujo – I even miss that sadistic dog.

I still dream. I still see myself doing mundane things like walking across a room, turning in a chair and my leg moving. I dream of rolling over, I dream of sleeping on my stomach. That's my favorite.

But in the meantime, I grab on to meg-leg and move it when it needs to be moved. I grin and grimace, but I do what I have to. Those muscles are going to remember. Hopefully tonight I dream of that day.

THINKING ABOUT BEING HOME FOR THE HOLIDAYS

I am a spectator in my life. Seeing pictures of my boys online for Thanksgiving instead of watching them from across the table. Listening to the banter on a phone 1200+ miles away instead of from the other room. Calls, texts, FaceTime all replacing human interactions.

I will be home this weekend. The journey will be uncomfortable and most likely painful, but I would crawl through glass at this point to be home.

I will not see my youngest for a few weeks after I arrive. He will be getting ready for finals and won't be able to come home until they are done.

The next milestone as a family will be Christmas. John and the boys do the heavy lifting. I place some interior decorations, but my main task is to decorate the tree, where I can reach.

John hates our ornaments. Well, not all of them. Most of them. We have gotten a new ornament every year we have been together. We have crappy ornaments from when we were in college. Cheesy just married ornaments. Cheap ornaments when we had no money. Various baby ornaments. Every glitter, popsicle stick, picture ornament the kids ever made. Crocheted snowflakes & bells (what's left that my dog did not eat) that my mom made for me when we moved to Florida, so I never missed snow. Ornaments that represent us – sports teams & movies & hobbies. That tree is a scrapbook of things I love. It won't be in any magazines and would probably make Martha Stuart vomit but it's beautiful to me. Each ornament I touch brings back a memory. Each touches my heart. They are the story of the best parts of my life.

But this year I will be a spectator as they do for me what I can not. I won't be able to stand and place these mementos on our tree. It's one more thing on my list of things to strive to do – next time.

Take to heart the message. Decorate the tree, bake the cookies, wear the pjs. Embrace the memories you are making because some day you may too be just a spectator.

TOMORROW, TOMORROW, TOMORROW

I keep thinking about tomorrow.

"Tomorrow and tomorrow and tomorrow, creeps in this petty place from day to day." Can't believe I still remember that from school.

Tomorrow, John is coming.

Tomorrow, is our Anniversary.

Tomorrow, I start to get ready to go home.

Tomorrow, we will relax and have dinner. The next day we will figure out how to pack my things. My things from my short vacation, my things that needed to be purchased for my unexpected extended stay, my things people sent me that helped me through the last few months, and my things that are now a part of my life (my adaptive tools). Sunday we will fly home.

I am getting butterflies in my stomach. I put my Ironman shirt on. This is what I have been waiting for. This is what I have been dreaming about. I wasn't planning on the wheelchair. There was a lot I was not planning for when I took off for vacation.

I'm not the planner, John is. He has gotten our home ready for what he believes I need. He has come up with multiple scenarios if his plan is off. He is still planning, trying to figure contingencies. He is planning for worse.

For better, for worse. In sickness and in health. He is planning for worse and for sickness. He doesn't see Ironman yet.

Divorce and separation in the US has been pretty steady at 50%. Thoughts of love and starting a family and happily ever after are very different from the realities of dirty diapers, juggling commitments, lawns that need mowing and laundry waiting to be washed. We make each other crazy, we yell, we hold hands, and we always kiss each other goodbye and good night.

Years ago, for our anniversary I wrote,

Love is…easy. Marriage is…hard. It takes work, dedication, commitment, and an understanding that vows are just not words. It should not be defined by the "Kodak Moments" of your time together, but rather be a culmination of all the smaller moments in between.

I listed a number of things John does in those smaller moments. Here I am again echoing the sentiment that vows are just not words.

For better, for worse. In sickness and in health.

We have had a lot of those moments too. Sitting in hospitals. Worse and sickness. This time it will not creep into our home, it will arrive in a wheelchair.

Know what else was in our vows? I will love you always.

TO JOURNAL OR NOT TO JOURNAL, THAT IS THE QUESTION

It's amazing how many people have reached out to see if I made it home safely, do we need anything, just "checking in" and a number of comments about the lack of journal posts and what does it means.

Yes, we made it home safely, no thank you we are good right now, thanks for checking, it means there are times I am getting to live my life, yet I am still on the journey. Being home brings some peace I have not had since the BOOM. I am reveling in the little things.

To recap what has transpired since last, I update you as follows:

The trip home was not as bad as the multiple scenarios in my head. I started the day by giving myself an injection in the stomach to prevent blood clots while flying. Another shot was to be administered the next day. Even a simple act of flying now has other consequences. Aside from the extensive searching, groping, and swabbing by TSA through security, the airline staff was most helpful. The general population not so much. My current handicap is letting me see the world from a new perspective- that of a wheelchair. I could not have navigated the airport on my own, and we would have struggled more without the assistance we received.

But a note to the others, there is a reason for special lines for wheelchairs and your total self-absorption made it unbelievably difficult for me and my fellow rolling travelers. Your disregard for the rules did not facilitate your travels, it just made it more difficult for us.

I also learned that not all handicap facilities are easily accessible by a wheelchair. I encountered a series of turns that cannot be done – the handicap facility mocking me on just the other side.

Leaving the airport was almost transcendental. The warm Florida breeze caressed my arms as if to welcome me home. I closed my eyes and smiled and reached out my arms like a child. I was home.

Walking into the house on my crutches I paused. What was so familiar I was now seeing through different eyes. My first reaction was how to navigate which surprised me. The therapists taught me well – my Karate Kid training kicked in without thought. The first afternoon and evening Home was exhausting. I somewhat settled into the guest room.

The next morning, I got to hug my son after months away. This big giant gave me the gentlest hug as if he did not know if I would break. Oh how I missed him. All I could think is I never want to be away from my family again.

Monday, I rested. The exhaustion of the last few months seemed to catch up with me. John and I are learning how to live with each other again after 28 years of marriage. All he wants to do is help. Ironman, however, is crashing her way through the house and knocking things down. I have to learn.

I learned I love my couch, but it is near impossible to get up from it on my own. It sits too low, and it is extremely painful when I try to rise. I learned I can sit at the table, but right now prefer to use the wheelchair I have been working so hard to get out of.

I learned I LOVE sleeping in a real bed. Being able to stretch my arms, the softness of the mattress on my ass tablet. Having room for my adaptive tools on the bed without worry of them falling on the floor. I sleep with almost everything I need. Someday they will be replaced by my husband. I wait for that day.

I practice while I have supervision. I practice most things I will need to be able to do on my own. I practice making coffee. Unbelievable number of "steps" but doable. I have cereal, I navigate the bathroom. There is not one thing I do simply the first time. My life is full of new firsts.

John and I do a dry run (lol) to figure out the best way to navigate the shower bench. Even the two-inch step out of the shower is insurmountable without crutches. We devise a plan. Success. I shower. A long, hot shower with no one taking me or helping me. I learn I will shower at night as it is time consuming and exhausting right now.

We went to the doctor for my follow-up care and second opinion. I am getting better in the car. I still white-knuckle hold onto the "oh my God" strap but am not having anxiety attacks every-time, anxiety yes, but I am breathing. There are no handicap spaces available and I tell John I can walk from the parking lot. We don't take the wheelchair as it is not meant for travel. It's a slow go, but we navigate to the doctor's office. Another success. I bring with me my abridged records and discs. I have over eight pounds of medical records so far.

This doctor is impressed by the handiwork of the trauma surgeon to the point I think he has a bit of a crush. He states right away I need the second surgery and walks though exactly why. He points out the areas on the films. It matches the NY surgeon.

He throws me for a loop as he wants to do the surgery soon. He explains where I am now is as good as I am going to get. The pain will only increase, and I will have no further improvements. He walks through two potential surgical plans depending on the next test results. I told him about not being able to completely use my leg. He asks me to do some basic movements. What I can do is only because I am compensating with other muscles. The hip does not work.

He looks at the films and he turns to me and says, "you are alive". He knows without being told about the BOOM how bad is was just by looking at these films and reading the surgical report. I now understand the reconstruction I had was needed based on the shattering. The next surgery is just to take me the final step of the way, pun intended. He lets me know the recovery will be nothing like what I just went though.

He says I can be walking a day or two after surgery with a walker. Walking. Full weight bearing walking. Walking, with a limp, but walking. This pain will be gone, as will the chair. He is right, there is no reason to wait. When I am cleared, I will have the surgery. There is no reason to continue on with this pain, with these limitations. We will try and plan for this in the new year. I should be dancing a jig by St Patty's Day. Well, maybe not dancing, but hopping and skipping along.

PS – this middle of the night update is brought to your courtesy of our dog. He came to check on me and woke me up by licking my hand. He has been sleeping predominantly by the side of my bed or in the hall just outside my door. I think maybe, secretly, he does love me.

TESTS

I had to go for a new test and to the doctor. The tables were turned as my son had to take me today, like I used to take him as a child. He too is trying. Trying to help. Trying to step back when he thinks I am asserting my independence. He is trying to figure me out. He is doing pretty well so far.

We arrived early for the CAT scan (not the only test today) as I still can't judge how long it takes me to get around. Then the technician ran behind. In the waiting room I was quizzed by another patient's wife. I saw her looking at me, trying to figure out my story. I need to get used to that. This too is a test; how will I deal with strangers. People by nature are inquisitive. I would rather someone look and ask, rather than sneak sideways stares. I am shuffling along on crutches at a snail's pace. Trying to sit or stand is not quick. I easily stand out in a crowd never mind a waiting room. I give her the 3-sentence abridged version. She tells me her husband fell in the house. I guess she felt the need to reciprocate. When they left, she wished me well and a full recovery. I believe she meant it.

When it was finally my turn, I went in. After the tech introduced herself, I explained my injury and limitations. She would need to lower the table. My shoe had to come off. She would need to lift my leg onto the table. She needed to move my crutches. She had to tie my feet together to get the right one to stay at the angle she needed. When done, she needed to untie my feet, help me up, get my shoe, get the crutches and lower the table again. The before and after took longer than the test. Another test, how will I remain patient when articulating my need for help. On to the next stop.

The doctor I needed to see is in the same building as dear friends. I texted ahead as we were going to be a bit early. I was going to be a surprise to most of the group. We parked and I walked around the small building to meet them. Again, still not looking my best, but I knew that didn't matter when I saw the look in their eyes when they saw me. Saw me standing on my crutches. This is another group of ladies I am blessed to know. The calls, texts, cards, notes, and care packages helped me, more than I can articulate properly, get through my rehab stay. It was not the gifts; it was the thought I could see and feel in each item they chose. They are the givers of my badass red, Ironman inspired, fingerless gloves that keeps the calluses at bay and give me strength. They were with me more than a thousand miles away. I could not thank them today, but I could hug each one. So, I did. Test – reconnecting.

Walked back around to the doctor. That went well. Off to home after driving through to pick up lunch. I make it into the house as my son brings in everything. I opt for the wheelchair. Test – knowing my limits.

We spend some time then he excuses himself. I decide I need to lie down for a bit. That tuned into a solid nap. If it weren't for a telemarketer and the need to use the restroom, I could have slept the day away. Test – how bad will the pain be when I am having a regular day. It is…manageable. My concern is the fact it will be increasing. We will address that next week.

I feel I passed all the tests today. There will be more tests in the days ahead. Tests I can't prepare for, can't anticipate, and never wanted.

Ironman out for the night.

I DROPPED MY CRUTCHES TODAY

I am now at the point of being left by myself for about 4 hours a day. I have been spending these last few days trying to figure out how to live in my house, how to prepare for returning to work, to learn my limits. I have been very careful not to put myself in a situation where I get stranded. At night I even make sure I take my cell phone in the bathroom in case I need to call for help. I have grabber tools in both the bed and family rooms.

I have been trying things. Getting in bed is perhaps the most painful task. I have tried different ways and angles to position my body and use the leg lifter to get meg-leg up on the mattress. Each try causes pain. Each try is exhausting. I generally gave up after three tries. But after a week I now have a method I can live with. It ain't fast nor is it pretty, but I cringe for only a few seconds. It will get me through until surgery.

I tried to empty the dishwasher. I won't be emptying the dishwasher. Not everything is a success story.

I binge watched The Voice. I am now all caught up.

Armed with the knowledge my hip did not heal properly I understand the pain I have is not something I should "work through". The "no pain no gain" mantra does not apply to me right now. I decided when sitting at the table I will use the wheelchair always. The table chairs do not have arms to support me when I stand. I can not turn easily in a regular chair. Both these actions cause pain. I can get into the kitchen with the chair, but I cannot get into the bedroom nor bathroom as it is too big. I use the crutches to get to the chair, and balance them on the table once I am situated.

I was sitting at the table making some calls and taking care of a few things. I went to move the crutches and oops. On the floor they went. My problem was the grabber was on the other side of the crutches. There was no way to get the chair around to get it. Tables and couches blocked my way. I can't easily bend or lean forward in the chair to pick things up. Without those crutches I am a prisoner. It took almost half an hour of using my good leg/foot and circus balancing to get my hands on one crutch. It only took about 5 minutes to get the second one.

Lesson learned. When I am by myself place the crutches on the other side of the table.

I PUT MY UNDERWEAR ON INSIDE OUT AND BACKWARDS

Tonight will be the first time all of my family will be under the same roof in ~4 months. My youngest son came home from college on winter break.

He drove home by himself, with a fellow student following in her car as she had no working GPS. Every parent knows that feeling deep in the pit of your stomach every time your child gets in a car. They are not safe until they are home. It doesn't matter if they are going for milk or driving across the state. He is responsible. He is a safe Driver. They are not safe until they are home.

Experiencing the BOOM exasperates that feeling. What I used to worry about I am now living through. I know firsthand it doesn't matter how safe or good a driver you may be, there are other Drivers on that same road you travel. I had him call when he was leaving, with a promise to call me from the road. I calculated his journey. I waited on a call that did not come. I stressed. I called him. He is safe; he is home.

I did not want the first time he saw me to be in that chair. I readied myself on my crutches so when he finally saw me it was upright. While I thought my oldest gave me the gentlest hug, this one was feather light. I looked at him and said I need a proper hug. His response was he does not want to hurt me; he didn't know where to hug or how hard.

I did not lie to my sons. I gave them the abridged version of what happened. As I was progressing in therapy, I thought I would get away with it. I thought there was a chance by the time I saw them again I could pass the BOOM off as just a big boo boo. I'm an ass sometimes.

As he was hugging me he stared at the wheelchair. ***sigh***.

I came clean a bit more. We went through the X-ray. I explained my current limitations. I went through how the downstairs is set up for me right now. I went through the need for the 2nd surgery and the possible timetable for that. We talked a little about the BOOM. It was enough for the first day.

I got in the chair and rolled up to the table. I made him catch me up on his first full semester away from home. We made time go lightly (love that song). He started his college student pile of laundry and things got back to normal(ish),

My muscles ache. I did not realize the tension I was causing in my body waiting for him to get home safely, waiting to see his reaction.

We watched tv after dinner until I knew I needed to get vertical. I need to use a dressing stick which is basically a stick of wood with hooks on the end. I need it to take off as well as put on anything below the waist. I can't bend and my right leg is still mostly for show.

The mind is very powerful. It realized he made it home safely. It realized we are all home. It realized the body was tired, achy, and sore. Time to get ready for bed (not sleep, just need vertical for now). Gathered clean clothes, toiletries, and dressing stick. Washed up and started to get changed. My underwear slipped off the stick. I stuck it, started over and then (sorry Northern friends) went to put on my shorts. Then I stood to pull them up. Finished dressing, brushed my teeth, and headed to bed but after a few steps – wait – something is just not right. The mind already checked out. A few more steps. Nope, back to the drawing board. Yup. Underwear on inside out and backwards. I'm an ass sometimes. Didn't even think to look how I scooped them up off the floor and reset them on the dressing stick. I was so confident in my skills with my adaptive tool I didn't pay close attention.

That got my attention. It was a simple mistake because I was complacent in this small task.

Yesterday I dropped the crutches. I am comfortable because I am home, but I have to make sure I am diligent and pay attention to what I am trying to accomplish. This small mistake caused me an additional 15+

minutes to remedy. It could have easily been a misstep with the crutches.

Tomorrow is a new day. A day I will have with my kids. I day I will be careful.

I AM ACHY

I have been making sure I am getting up early, getting dressed, and sitting as much as I can. I am building my stamina living back in the real world. I am trying my best to forgo the midday naps. I am trying to use the crutches more and more. I even tried the dishwasher again. Ended up dropping a crutch. I can't do the f'ing dishwasher.

Today was a busy day. My eldest took me out after he went to get my handicap placard. At his suggestion we made some modifications to me getting in and out of the car. His suggestions hurt less so that's a win. I went to get a haircut. Guess what? No available handicap spots. Of course, it's my luck. He dropped me off and I went in while he parked. I glanced around, no seat had arms. I was concerned to try and sit unaided. I stood until he came in. He then had to help me up and then down in the salon chair. It took all of 5 seconds before I was asked what happened. Hopefully only a few more months of that. Sitting in the chair was uncomfortable as I had to put both feet on the step bar which caused an angle the made the bones grind together. I calculated how long it would take and sucked it up.

When we were done, we ran another errand. Guess what? No available handicap spots. I am getting my moneys worth out of my parking placard. This time I walked from the parking lot. I walked and stood and finally sat for a few minutes in the store. When done we went back to the car. Someone had parked closer on the passenger side which prohibited me from getting in the car. My son saw I was getting tired and finally pulled the car out in the road and looked at me and said everyone will have to wait 2 minutes. My boy.

We came home and I wanted a nap. But I did not give in. The surgeon's office called to remind me of my appointment tomorrow and let me know the elevator is broke. I will have to do the stairs on my crutches. I am living Ground Hogs Day.

My youngest and I watched some cooking shows and then started on trimming the tree. The boys set the tree itself up yesterday. I pulled up my chair and offered suggestions. We talked about a few ornaments. The kid had it, he has a good eye. I took a bathroom break and when I came back he looked at me and said I saved some for you to put on. He saved a handful of the snowflakes and bells my mother made for me. I got up from the chair and on my crutches got closer to the tree. I sidestepped around and was able to place the small number. I was unsteady and the aches were setting in. But I held in my hands what my mother had made for me with love, which was handed to me by my son with the same love. He knows what they mean to me. He had already gotten on a stepladder and down on his knees to do all the other ornaments. He placed the homeless family (nativity scene) under the tree. He then went to place other decorations around the downstairs. Not the way I would have done it, but I let him go. Again, the kid has a good eye and everything so far looks great. We will finish tomorrow. PS: he also loaded, ran, and emptied the dishwasher.

John came home and the four of us had dinner together. They selected a movie but the day had gotten to me. I need to be vertical and try and rest because there will be a lot of stairs tomorrow, and probably no handicap spaces.

***side note; after John had left for work and both the boys were still sleeping, I did hang another ornament, a gift. It's Ironman. ***

WEEKEND IS OVER

It's odd how the days are going by so quickly and dragging at the same time. My down time has been just that – lying down on a bed. The limitations are frustrating. Home is a million times better than rehab, but I'm still a prisoner. I can't go out on my own. The few times I have been outside the house have been due to necessity. The ever-present swelling is getting old. While I am still reveling in a hot shower someone needs to be downstairs just in case. The more I get the more of my life I want back.

Tomorrow, I return to work, albeit from home for a bit. My brain has been on overdrive thinking about all I want to get done. Realistically it will take days to get my security back and look through emails. It's a start. Yet like everything else I am calculating.

I have scheduled my next surgery. For a change there is good news – the bones have healed enough that I will be having a less invasive technique performed. It means adding yet another scar to my long growing list, but it significantly reduces the recovery time. Also good is that almost all of the new hardware will be staying. To do the next surgery it looks like only one screw will have to be removed. The surgeon was again amazed at how much of my brokenness held together and how well I have healed.

The bone that shifted has caused the top of the femur to die and to not be able to go into the right place. The femoral head has collapsed. Right now, what I can do is as good as it is going to get until surgery. The pain will continue, and meg-leg will not work. There is no reason to postpone the surgery. The quicker I can get it done the quicker I will be walking.

I am calculating what I can get done before the second surgery. I have outlined my work plan, but it's more than that. I will visit with friends I have not seen in months. I will have holidays with my family. I will make sure the dog gets his shots. I will deal with all of the pre-op testing. I will renew my prescriptions. I will fill my days and nights with living a normal life.

But I will also make sure a list of all my logins and passwords and contacts are updated. I will have all of the insurance information together. I will make sure next semester's charges are all paid in full. I will start a file for our taxes. I will be able to plan for someone else to pick up the ball if I cannot. I wasn't able to do that before and I'm not taking any chances. It's an odd feeling when someone, no matter how close, has to go through your things and try and pick up your life.

I LOVE WORKING

Boy, that's something I never would have said before the BOOM. I went to work daily because; college is expensive lol. As is insurance, car loans, mortgage…you get the idea. If we were ever to hit the big lottery and I could retire I planned on being a volunteer that holds babies in hospitals. But my real plan was to work until I die (see sentences 2 & 3 again). But a head on collision later and work was not my priority. My priority was getting out of that bed. Learning: to dress myself, to use the bathroom, to navigate in a wheelchair, to use crutches, to shower, to make a cup of coffee. My priority is walking. My priority is my family.

But I worried that months of geriatric companions, daytime TV (especially my roommate's fondness for the Game Show Network), and doing therapy to the point of exhaustion would chip away at what I do and in some part who I am. To say I have not been changed by this would be a lie. I am two days in, and everything came back like raging flood waters. I was so engulfed I skipped lunch the first day. All I had to do was wheel myself 10 feet, but I did not stop.

My team let me know I had been missed. But was I needed? Yes. I had several calls and emails as soon as people saw I was online. They all started the same way, how are you, glad you are back, etc. Then, I need….can you look at this…we need to talk. I've updated the budget, reviewed some spreadsheets, dealt with HR and have 75% of mandatory training done. This transition week let's everyone know I am ok; I can still do my job. The slow shuffle in the office next week will now be secondary. I'm back.

Even though I am at home I am trying to replicate what it will be like in the office. I need to calculate when do I need to get up to stretch, to walk a few steps. I don't have it down pat yet. I've got an achy pain that's not going away. Like everything I do I have to figure it out by trial and error. Right now, I am a bit heavier on the error side, but it will come.

One step at a time.

Ironman.

I AM CONTENT

That's a word that people don't throw around much anymore, it's said like it's a bad thing. Are you content enough to....? (Add anything here – stay in that job, date that guy, keep that car). I'm not sure why being content is no longer enough.

To be content means to be in a state of peaceful happiness.

Several of our friends came over this weekend to visit. We caught up, had pizza, drinks and dessert and ongoing laughs.

Tomorrow when I wake up, my children, my husband and I will have Christmas breakfast together. That is a gift 4 months ago I would not have asked for, but it hands down the beats any other I will receive.

The following day I will head into the office, the first time since September. It will be great to see and thank people in person who have been cheerleading my recovery. I learned who are people with whom I just work and people who have come to care for me. It is rare to be in a position to learn that.

Normal. I am having a mostly normal week.

My new normal includes difficulty getting in and out of bed, pain in my leg and hip, discomfort when I sit or lay down, and oh yeah, still having that walking issue.

Yet I am content. I have learned (the hard way) there are infinite things that are not in my control. This week I can harp on those and the position I am in, or I can enjoy reconnecting and spending the holidays with my family. I choose the latter. I choose to be happy.

Christmas embodies giving and sharing love and reaching out to those who have touched our lives. I count my blessings and am grateful to have come this far and for all who have touched my life. I wish for you the best of Christmas.

23 DAYS – HOPEFULLY

That's how long it is until my next (hopefully last) surgery. I have been counting down since the doctor's visit.

24 Days. That's the countdown until I can (hopefully) walk without this pain.

I have not abandoned this journal, this outlet that helped keep me sane in an otherwise insane set of circumstances. I'm just tired, very tired; and trying to make the most of my time with my family. My son goes back to college in less than a week. Again, I will not be able to visit for quite some time. (Hopefully) maybe he will be able to make at least a weekend visit home. I just want to hug my kids and never let them go.

I went back into the office this past week. Again, more figuring out how to make things work. It was good to properly thank those who have been in my corner in person. Those who truly care come to check on me throughout the day – bearing snacks and drinks and more importantly friendship. I will admit to bouts of emotion at times.

I had a steady stream of visitors most who stated the same three sentences:

1. With a surprised face, "You look good". I think half of them were expecting me to show up with some sort of exoskeleton or at least in the wheelchair. They don't know how hard I worked busting my ass not to have to use that chair unless absolutely necessary. Also my new set of scars are not visible with pants on (partly with shorts). The ancillary cuts and bruises have since faded. While I am not fast on these crutches, I am vertical. I have been busting ass for over 3 months now. The swelling is my constant companion with its friend grey and falling out hair. I am shedding more than the dog.

The anesthesia and stress from the injury and surgery has lasting effects. Which will get extended after the next surgery. (Hopefully) by April/May I should see improvements.

2. "It's good to see you". My response is "it's good to be seen". That is not a flippant answer, I truly mean it. The alternative was not so good.

3. "Why don't you just get a motorized wheelchair? It would be so much easier". No, no it won't. While I would be able to get from place to place quicker, the more time I spend in that chair the more progress I am

undoing. I need to keep the muscles that can work hard at work. I need to continue with upper body strength as I need it daily to get dressed, get in and out of bed, to get up from a chair…I could go on. I need to be vertical to try and keep the spasms at bay. I need not go backwards even a foot as this progress will (hopefully) aide in how quick I can recover from the next surgery. In life there is the right way and the easy way. Right way all the way.

By the evening I was spent. I was in bed before 8 most nights. As meg-leg is still useless I cannot bend or move it during the night which causes stiffness and spasms. I am still getting up every 2-3 hours. It is taxing to get up out of bed when all I want to do is roll over and sleep. I tried again, unsuccessfully. (Hopefully) I should be able to do so 2 months after my surgery. When all is done it will be ~6 months since I was able to roll over in bed.

I have taken a muscle relaxer today, the first in several weeks. I have come to tolerate the level of pain I now have and am very diligent to avoid movements where I know the pain will be astronomical (learned the hard way- lol). The tightness of the muscles has been pushing the bad bones and I do not want to enter the New Year in additional discomfort. My mom used to tell me whatever New Year's brings sets the tone for your upcoming year. Not going to jinx it. I will be surrounded by my family when we say goodbye to this year and bring in the New (and hopefully better) Year.

Christopher Reeve said "once you choose hope anything is possible"

I am not so naive to think all things are just going to be sunshine and unicorns. I am relying on hope to see me through this continued journey. To see possibilities and opportunities in challenges, not that there will be no challenges at all. To live this life with no hope would lead me into a downward spiral, a path I am not going to take.

So please take this as my hope for you in the New Year.

I HAD A SMALL PANIC ATTACK TODAY

John was driving me to work at the crack of dawn today. He has been very good about driving slower than he would like as he knows that while I am much better, being in a car is still tough. We were on I95 when I watched as a man veered into our lane – on my side. There were cars in the lane to our left and John had very little room to maneuver safely which thank God he was able to do. The man didn't even look at us – he just looked down as he kept driving and rubbed his head. He knew he screwed up and didn't have the nerve to acknowledge his actions.

All I saw was a car heading straight towards me and I couldn't move. I tensed so much that I felt the bone hit bone and saw stars. It was just a few seconds – but so was the BOOM. I didn't realize my hand was holding on so tight that I still have pain hours later. Then the small panic attack set in. I looked out the window, so John did not see how bad it was, but he knew something. He spoke in a calm voice telling me this is natural because I was in a horrible accident. Thank you, Mr. Obvious. It made me chuckle. He did not see me cry in the dark of the morning. I was doing much better – until today.

My ass tablet is killing me so much tonight that I have dipped into the pain killers and muscle relaxers I have been saving (because I don't know how much worse the pain will be before I can be operated on).

***Note: due to new laws to curtail the opioid crisis I am in a catch 22 until my next surgery. NY Rx's cannot be filled in Fl. The Fl surgeon can't write an Rx because he did not do the surgery. The pain clinic would not take my 8+ pounds and 6 cds of medical records because they are from NY. My new Fl tests are also not enough without a written referral from my Fl doctor – who won't write one because if the pain clinic screws up, he could lose his license. They all agree I have a still broken hip and a collapsed femoral head and am experiencing a high level of pain. They all apologize too and state I am not the person these laws were written for, but I am the person getting screwed. I looked into medical marijuana, but it takes a month. I will be walking by then. Hopefully, there is that word again. ***

I am used to the pain as I keep my "when I really need them, I will take them" remaining meds safely put aside. It has been tolerable, I am used to it, I am Ironman – until today. Physically and emotionally, I am back several months.

But tomorrow I will wake to the dawn of a new day. I will have breakfast and spend some time with my son before he heads back to school.

To better days ahead. To 19 days and counting.

GOOD GOES TO HEAVEN BAD GOES TO HELL AND OTHER THINGS I THINK

This is my mantra since the BOOM. For non-PT readers it is a reminder of how you are to step to be safe. Good leg is always the one that goes up first. Bad is always the one that goes down first. Not following this order can be extremely detrimental, aside from pain I could severely injure myself. It's been 116 days and I say this to myself every time I need to lift a foot. I do it without thinking it has become so second nature – to be safe.

But today I thought about it. I have a two-inch step for the shower. I said it getting in, and I said it getting out. Then today I thought, will there ever be a day I can take a step and not hear this in my head?

I hate that it is 116 days later and I am not still able to go one day without a reminder. I am 10 days away from surgery and hopefully 11 days away from walking. Then another 6 weeks with precautions. Who knows how long after until I can finally roll over and sleep. I think about these things every day too. Each day that passes I recalculate the next part of my life. Every day.

I think about the fact that I have not looked at my scar in its entirety. I feel it every day. I massage it to try and lessen the pins and needles, try different ointments to sooth the muscle ache. I can tell you the areas where I have not gotten feeling back. But I can't tell you what it looks like. 111 days since my surgery and I still haven't seen the entire scar. I'm sure there is a therapist out there who would love to tell me why.

I think my husband looks tired, no he is tired. It's more than having to take on all the additional burdens of everyday life. The sound of my crutches or the movement of my wheelchair has him up in an instant. It's been 116 days since he has had a restful night. As much as I try to be independent is as hard as he fights to do everything. We remain at an impasse. It's like we are facing off at opposite ends of a battlefield. In between us lays our hearts so we tread lightly. It is a war we fight every day, but one neither wants.

I think about how roles have been reversed and now my son drives me to appointments. How every time before he leaves me to go upstairs, he asks "Do you need anything momma?" Since I'm home he has not called me just mom. I think how I am downplaying my next surgery to him and am I being fair? It's not just him, I say with a smile to everyone it's a simple fix with just some more titanium being added.

It it supposed to be a piece of cake after everything I've been through, but I think about the secret file I have that has all the passwords, websites, insurance information all in one place should anything happen. Someone will tell John where to find it should it ever be needed.

I think about I may have to say "Good goes to heaven, Bad goes to hell" every day for the rest of my life. I think I am scared the surgery may not work.

"FALLING AND GETTING BACK UP IS WHAT BRINGS YOU SUCCESS." TONY HORTON

I fell yesterday. There was water on the floor hidden in the grout line after the floor was cleaned and my crutch caught it just right. Panic set in and I was able to pivot and go down on my non operative side.

I was home alone. Stuck on the floor with a leg I can't move. I waited a few minutes and took stock of any injuries. Ass tablet in no worse shape, soreness where my body broke the fall. I crawled to my crutch to get my phone from the handy crutch pocket. I called John, sounding all phony chipper to see when he would be home. Then I let him know I was ok but fell and was stuck on the floor.

I will be the death of him.

Add to that the number of pre-op testing I am having and it hasn't been a good week. So far, I am not cleared for surgery. I am now waiting on one last test that will be the make or break if I can stay on schedule for next week.

If the answer is no, I need to get a wheelchair for work, I can't continue on much longer – it's harder than I thought. The wheelchair I have is oversized and made to coddle my injury site, not to move around and live your forever life. If I don't have the surgery next week it will be a bigger fall than the one I had yesterday. Yesterday's fall resulted in visible bruising – postponing surgery will have deep but invisible wounds. That fall will be hard to get up from.

I'm so close. One week. To be decided by *one test*.

SATURDAY MORNINGS

When I was little Saturday mornings meant we could eat cereal as we sat in front of the tv. When the kids were little Saturday mornings were spent rushing and going to some kind of sport they were involved in. When I got older Saturday mornings meant I could sleep in – let myself recoup from whatever the week had thrown at me – recharge my batteries.

Saturday mornings since the BOOM have been like every other morning since the BOOM. My leg tightens and spasms and causes me enough discomfort that I have to get up. If I am lucky, I can get 3 hrs uninterrupted sleep during the night.

It is physically not easy to get up and it's still painful. I have slept with adaptive tools next to me for over well over 100 days, without them I am glued to wherever I am.

I am tired.

I am done.

I am cleared for surgery.

As I struggled this morning, I thought of Saturday mornings past (pre-BOOM), I remembered flashes of running to be the first to the tv (you got to choose the channel), of rushing to make sure the boys had their mouth guards before we left, of rolling over and tucking myself back in the covers for a few more hours.

Will this be my last Saturday morning of hooking a leg lifter on meg-leg and painfully dragging it to the side? Of having to brace myself for the shot of pain as I struggle to stand with the crutches? Of trying to massage the spasms away?

Counting down.

A LITTLE MORE THAN A DAY TO GO…

Yet still having tests done. The hospital called to say they require an additional blood test. The cardiologist wants to check me one more time. They are having me "run around town" when it's all I can do to make it in from the car. My bag is not packed yet. I don't know what time my surgery is scheduled for.

I'm so over everything.

The surgeon alleviated my panic somewhat, he is so sure of the surgery. He set expectations of what will be required of me after the surgery – the work I need to do to ensure success. *He has no idea.* He doesn't see Ironman. He talks about walking within weeks. He is the only doctor through this entire ordeal that has not sat with me and told me what the worst could be. He speaks only of walking.

Walking. I will be walking in a few weeks. I know I will have to push myself. I know it will still be a while before I can roll over and sleep. I know I will do whatever it takes to get back in my feet.

13 HOURS

I am at the point where I am no longer counting down the days, but the hours. I am less than 13 hours away from surgery. My mind is playing these last few months like a movie in fast forward.

BOOM. It used to start with the BOOM. Not tonight though. I started back a few days before, for my LLBFF's party. Knowing now what the outcome of my trip turned out to be, would I have stayed behind?

No, at least today I don't think so. Don't get me wrong, I could have done without the broken ass tablet and all that came with it. But life is meant to be lived, to be enjoyed, and especially to be celebrated. I would not have missed celebrating her birthday for the world. How could I have not been there with her when she has been with me at so many pivotal times in my life?

I've told this story before. My father died when I was 14. My memories have faded through the years, but several remain strong. Going to the zoo or horseback riding, stopping in the neighborhood bar on the way home to get a coke that had maraschino cherries filled to the rim (today he would have probably gotten arrested for bringing me in lol). Most of all I remember the Yankee games. Watching him walk down the street after getting off the train from work, only to head right back with me to catch a game. He loved going to the ballpark. I loved going with him. I hold the Yankees in my heart with my dad. I left home with very few things under not the best circumstances. I have a handful of pictures and aside from those, all I have are the times that stick out in my mind. I never thought he would be gone before I realized how much I needed him. Fourteen years was nothing.

When John and I decided to start a family, I knew I would fill the kids' days with memories so if someday I was not around they would not have to struggle to remember. It was years of going to games, being team mom, getting a fort for the yard, a multitude of pets (and being the one to pick up mice to feed the snakes). I even got my first tattoo a few years ago with my oldest son. I will continue to fill their days anytime I have an opportunity (& they let me). Whenever it is that I am no longer here, my children will never not know, not feel, the love I have for them.

Continuing along those lines there was no way I would have missed that celebration. Sometimes the best thing you can do is just be there.

What else would have happened had I not gone? There is so much I would not have learned.

I learned how truly blessed I am. Others may go a whole lifetime not knowing the love and support I have received these last few months. What a gift!

I have learned how to appreciate the little things I took for granted (like being able to sleep on your stomach – someday).

I think back on my days in rehab and how much I hated it. But I also remember the dance parties. I learned you have to have fun and celebrate all your successes.

I reconnected with people who were meaningful at different times in my life. I learned they are still meaningful.

I still don't know why I was unlucky enough to be in the BOOM. But an anger at God has now strengthened my faith.

On the eve of the day of a surgery I pray lets me walk again, I am ok.

Love to you all and much thanks for continuing on this journey with me.

A VIEW FROM THIS HOSPITAL BED

Surgery was yesterday. Unfortunately, the hospital ran behind, so it was delayed which kept me in bed yesterday.

When I woke in the recovery room I obviously felt like crap. There was a new pain where the surgery took place, but not the pain that has been my constant companion. Still pain, but in this case different was better.

The doctor came by to let me know everything went well and asked me to wiggle my toes. Different day, same drill. But this time I couldn't move my right foot at all. "ok" he said, "I'll be back".

Nurses then came over with warming blankets that now blocked my view of my foot. I started to think that this sure thing was maybe not so much of a sure thing. The surgeon kept coming back, but we had the same outcome.

Finally, I moved, and we all breathed a sigh of relief. I had a combination of anesthesia one of which was an epidural which apparently did not wear off as quickly as anticipated. We waited as there were no rooms available.

I was moved. It was a quick but rough move to the bed. This time I am in a private room. Things are looking up. John comes in, I am groggy and still feel like crap but am happy to see him.

He tells me he met with the surgeon who told him he had a hard time evening up my legs. When he measured, he came up one way, when he x-rayed another. He called an audible and used the physical measurement.

Later he would tell me he had no pre-BOOM pictures to go by and why he selected the measurement he did – to help me walk better. This was the first discussion of walking post surgery. He will see me this morning and I will start therapy around 9 to learn how to walk. He is still confident that once the muscles remember I will be walking unaided in several weeks. I could hug him.

The nausea was bad, but I needed something in my stomach to offset the meds. Jello to start, then John went and got me some ginger ale and plain cake. They brought up a dinner tray – which turned my stomach more. Not horrible, just not for me, but it did have a flower on the dish. That's the difference when you are in a Boca hospital. They came by and took my breakfast order, big menu to choose from (exactly like rehab – not!).

I've had people in and out of my room all evening and morning just like every hospital, but all of them were extremely pleasant. They walk me though what they are doing and why and ask what I need. They all talk about a good recovery. Finally, at 4 a.m. someone asks about what happened. I tell the story yet again, and she holds my hand. "You will be fine" she says as she looks me in the eye.

I will be fine.

BONUS UPDATE

The doctor and his assistant came by. He explained all of the follow-up he needs to do as I now have a massive amount of hardware. He is very excited for me to come in the office and see the X-rays (I am too). He is worried about the amount of bone I have right now, so he added 4 new screws and ended up not taking any out after all. The hope is the bone grows around the new implants as well as it is starting to grow around the ass tablet.

We spoke about my knee pain which he said is to be expected as they hammer the stem into your leg. Ah, ok.

PT came and I got out of bed and used the walker with some assistance and went past the hospital desk and back (maybe around 50 feet). I stood on 2 legs. I have not done that since September 19. My first foray out on my new hip was surreal. It was clunky and slow, and I held onto the walker for dear life. But I stood and used my right leg. This is going to work, I am going to be able to walk in a few weeks, I am certain. I am emotional to be experiencing something I have been only dreaming about. Today is a great day!

I'VE BEEN UP SINCE 5:15 AM

I have had the most un-interrupted sleep last night since the BOOM. Four- and one-half hours of solid sleep, no muscle spasms and no pain (thanks to the painkillers). The nurse had me up and I decided to stay up and start my day. Bathroom, washed, and got dressed. I still have to use the adaptive tools until the muscles wake up. But I was able to perform the tasks quicker and with none of the previous pain. Surgical pain is still there but treatable.

The surgeon came by, and we discussed the still nonfunctioning muscles. He reiterated it will be somewhere between 1-2 weeks but when they wake up – he can't wait! He can't wait?! This guy cracks me up. If I pass PT today, I go home later this afternoon. I got this. Doc says I look too good to be in a hospital. That's because Ironman is in the f'ing house!

Bandages were changed – I can't believe how great the new surgical area looks – helluva lot better than the first one still looks.

Walking will be my best therapy. I will have to have a minimum of 2 walks a day, as much as I can tolerate. That will force the muscles to move and start to get the prosthetics to adhere and stimulate bone growth. The swelling is not horrible today but is expected to get out of control fast the more I move. I still have my collection of granny panties and extra big shorts to fit over the hip so I'm good.

They did a strength assessment and were very pleased. As much as the crutches were sucking the very life force out of me, they were correct that it would keep up my strength and facilitate this recovery. I will learn some new strengthening exercises today for the muscles needed to use the walker. Still, none of these exercises will bring me closer to Michelle Obama arms but I could definitely win my share of arm wrestling.

I have to think when I move that I can put full weight on my leg. The doc and the therapists say overcoming the fear will be a challenge. I find myself starting to favor the leg and have to stop and reset. Old dog, new trick.

I also have to give a shout out to the support staff in this hospital. After the nightmares I endured this was a wonderful place to start the finish of my journey. The staff is pleasant and attentive. They continue to check on me throughout the day. My comfort is their concern. Smiles abound as do positive energy. The bosses come in several times a day to make sure the staff is meeting my needs. The nurses are gentle and the aides are super helpful. Even the food staff is amazing, and the food is edible. I wish you could smell the French Toast.

Can't wait to get back on my feet this morning. It's going to be a good day.

I CRIED IN FRONT OF JOHN THIS MORNING

Since the BOOM I have had more than enough tears and breakdowns to last a lifetime. However, I tried my best to keep it together in front of my loved ones (not 100% successful but I did my best). Could not stop the waterworks this morning.

I got home yesterday. Walked in the house on 2 feet with the walker. Slow and clunky and holding on for dear life, but upright and on my own. I was tired and took it easy for the remainder of the day. Saw both my boys (albeit for a short period) as my youngest came home for the weekend with friends and the older one has work.

It was a good night, I slept on the recliner and had zero spasms and pain. Only have taken 1 painkiller since I'm home. This surgical pain is nothing compared to what I have been living with.

This morning I am again trying to navigate my new normal. I walked a bit, got washed and changed and decided to try my luck sitting in a real chair – not the wheelchair which has been my constant home companion. I moved a plain wooden kitchen chair and gingerly lowered myself on it. It is still difficult making certain movements.

Then I waited. I waited for the pain. I waited for the discomfort. I waited for the ever present need to shift. I waited for the feeing that I was sitting on something. Nothing. Nothing happened. Then I cried. Boo hoo hold your hands to your face crying. John had no idea what was happening. Through my tears all I could say is I have no pain.

The nurse will be here soon to check on me, still no word on the PT. I will continue my small walks around the house. Unfortunately, it will be raining for a few days so my trip down the driveway will have to wait for now.

I am overcome. I have no words. I am on a path to walking.

I expect to be writing a lot more updates.

EXERCISES AT 2 A.M.

I fell asleep 2x on the couch tonight. I am exhausted. The nurse came today, and I can take care of myself, so she won't be back. The PT came and we spent a good deal of time together, mostly assessing my background, injuries, the house, and Ironman in general. She will be back Tuesday.

For the type of surgery I had (anterior), the PT is relatively simple:

- More and short rather than long walks. To the door and back works for now as I still get winded.

- Isometric exercises every hour I am sitting and awake. These 3 exercises suck the life out of me for as simple they are.

- Ice.

- Elevate.

- Stay ahead of the pain.

I awoke from my current sleeping situation due to the call of nature. I could use some ice. I am by myself downstairs and tired – I will skip rather than trying something I may not be able to do in the middle of the night. I have some pain. But the sick feeling in my stomach is still there. The pain meds will make it worse, and this is tolerable compared to what I had. I will skip.

So after my short walk to the bathroom, I am back on the couch in limbo. I am making up for the exercises I missed while I was sleeping. I could use ice. I could use a painkiller.

I GOT THE ICE AND TOOK A PAINKILLER DURING THE NIGHT

It didn't matter I was downstairs by myself; I was hitting a wall. I also had a soda to help with the continued upset stomach. Things that you truly believe can be changed in an instant – at 2ish there was no way *I* was getting up. By 3 there was no way I was not getting ice and a painkiller.

For some reason that 360 turn reminded me of how bad I am with dates. John had our wedding date inscribed inside my ring that's how bad I am with remembering. I am just as bad with names. Yet when the PT questioned me yesterday, I was able to spit out the dates of the BOOM and the surgery quicker than I could my own children's birthdays. That is how much I am seeing the BOOM has defined who I am now.

I spent part of the morning going back through previous days writings all the way back to the beginning. This has been a hell of a journey. One I feel is coming down to the home stretch. I am so close – but not there yet. I've already done 3 sets of exercises and 2 walks today. I have to make sure I push hard uphill to the finish. The swelling is setting in according to schedule. I will shower later today. I will do what I have to do. I will continue on like I started as I reflect on where I am now.

I read and reread how this BOOM will not define me, but I am _sure_ it has now, it _is_ now. It is defining me as much as getting married, the birth of my sons, the death of my sister. It seeps into every aspect of my life and those close to me. Except now it defines success. It defines hope. It defines spirit and love and pain. It defines the best and the worst. It defines a life worth living and fighting for.

WALKING IS HARD WORK

Did you catch that? _WALKING IS HARD WORK_!!!!!

It ain't pretty, but I am shuffling along. **_I am standing on my own fucking two feet_** (walker assist)!

*** appropriate use of f bomb if ever it was needed. ***

Swelling super crazy. Pins and needles down to my foot as the nerves are starting to wake up more each day. Pain pre this surgery – gone! This surgical pain – very tolerable considering. I have more discomfort from the swelling than the surgical area. The worst will be this week and will most likely take several months to fully resolve. Been there, done that. Actually, the swelling never went all the way away as the bones were so out of whack. Ice is my friend.

Last night I was able to get into bed without using a leg lifter for the first time. I sat on the bed and was able to scooch back and lift my leg enough to get in. Last time I did that? September 18. No pain when I did it. Would you like me to repeat that? NO PAIN.

PT came today. After my exam and exercises, we went outside. Took a walk to my neighbor's house and back. It took 12 minutes. To walk next store. You know what? I'll take that.

She stated how well I am progressing (Ironman) then proceeded to give me more to do. ***sigh*** OK I can do it.

She likes my little old lady pouch attached to the walker. I explain I always want to make sure I have a phone handy. No need to go into detail why.

She states I have to work on a more normal gait. I stop and hold. Then walk. I remind her I have not walked in months. I am unsteady. These muscles have yet to remember. Also, my knee is killing me. I have all the excuses. I also tell her maybe I am afraid. Yes, to all she says. Practice practice practice. I have to stand in the kitchen in front of the sink and then let go. If I feel myself slipping just grab back on. It's confidence and memory as much as strength. She checks my swelling again before she leaves. She checks my ankles and feet to ensure a good pulse. We discussed my kindergarten inspired PT shoelaces. Elastic with a clip. I tell her I had to loosen them 2x today. Hopefully it won't be too much worse she says. I appreciate honesty.

But I'm done. I'm tired from today. The swelling is continuing to get worse and putting a lot of pressure on the hip. I took a painkiller, my first one of the day. I'm no hero and I know when I need them. I am in bed. My recovery will continue to impose limits. But that's ok. For tomorrow I walk again.

"THIS HAS TO BE THE WORST THING EVER THAT HAPPENED TO YOU"

A simple statement, not made maliciously, nor waiting on any confirmation. Surely this BOOM and everything with it had to be the worst. I didn't know how to respond. The quick, flippant answer was "it wasn't one of the best."

Yet I am thinking about both the statement and my response tonight.

I'm not using this as a political or religious forum – what I write is first and foremost for me, to help make sense of this journey. It's for others, that maybe some understanding to know you are not alone may help on a dark day. It's for my cheerleaders to help them keep in step with me. But I started this saying I would be honest. So here goes.

I have been watching and reading the news all week. The fact that there are celebrations for allowing pregnancies to be terminated all the way through the 9th month is turning my stomach. I am going to make several statements; I am Christian, yet I am Pro-choice. My choice, my belief does not negate what someone else may be going through. I firmly believe in a woman's right to choose. I am blessed with two wonderful sons. Yet I was pregnant three times. I miscarried a child. Note I say a child. I lost a child. No one will ever be able to tell me differently. For years I would be sad around the time I should have been celebrating another birthday, then even sadder when the year came that I forgot. Unless you have been through it there are no words that can describe that loss. I had a dog at the time that if you ask anyone was more trouble than he was worth. There was nothing I wouldn't do for that dog, partly because he was so dumb you had to love him, but truthfully because when I was going through what I thought was the worst thing to ever happen to me, he crawled in my lap as I sat on the floor. When it was all over and I couldn't bear to talk to anyone, this dog felt my loss and stayed with me.

Then my sister got cancer. At that point we were living over a thousand miles apart. I made as many trips as I could. For general visits, special doctors' appointments, new treatment plans, and finally just a goodbye trip. Over the course of a year, I watched as the person who held so much of my heart wasted away and suffered. I was at work late one night when I got the call from the ER asking what choice I was to make as I was the health proxy. They needed an answer now, on the phone. There was no waiting to get there. I gave them the answer she wanted – DNR. It was a few days before Thanksgiving with a snowstorm crippling the East Coast. Only through a dear friend was I able to get connecting flights taking me several hours away from my final destination. I was able to arrange to be picked up in a snowstorm and driven to the hospital in the middle of the night. The nurse told me she let her know I was on the way. She told me she was waiting for me. She never regained consciousness as I crawled into her bed and said my goodbyes. In the morning we left her room as the doctor examined her. He came out to say it would be within a few hours. She had a different idea. She passed when he walked out of the room. I went through trains, planes, automobiles, and storms for my sister to die in her room alone. I was broken for a very long time. Surely this was the worst thing that ever happened to me.

You all know the story of this BOOM. Worst thing that ever happened to me?

I say yes and no to all. All three of these events broke me somehow. All three shook my faith. All three very truly horrific events make up my nightmares. All three events have left me with triggers that bring me back – to the floor, to the hospital room, to the car. I most certainly would give almost anything to have skipped any or all of them.

The child I lost may have never felt sun on its face or got to play with that stupid dog, but I believe its soul is living its best life. There is a phrase – "a rainbow baby", one born after such a loss as mine. It represents hope after the storm. I say my first son is my heart, but my second is my soul. His kindness and gentleness are gifts for which I am thankful for daily. I am blessed by my sons. If I had not suffered this loss, would my second son, my rainbow baby, ever come to be? I can't imagine my life without him.

When words were getting hard towards my sister's end, I sent her a copy of Winnie the Pooh as it said so many things I could not articulate. I still flip through the pages on days when I miss her.

"How lucky I am to have something that makes saying goodbye so hard."

The support I received after her passing remains unparalleled. The group of women who for almost a year helped me pick up the pieces went from friends to my sisters. If I were never to see any of them again, my love and gratitude would not diminish. That is how much they changed my life.

The BOOM. Yesterday I walked to the end of the driveway and back with a cane. The PT was holding onto the back of my pants just shy of giving me a wedgie as I teetered along. I was exhausted and spent. We will try the cane again next week. While not horrific, the pain increased. I looked like I was 90. And I was as happy as a pig in shit. I walked to the end of the driveway. I am looking at Badass canes – Dragons and the like should it turn out that I will need one long term. It is only a matter of time when I walk – when I take that first step unaided. How lucky am I! I was again blessed; to have surgeons who were able to piece together the parts of me and screws and plates and prosthesis enough that I am standing. Should I have had a lesser surgeon (for either operation) walking would not be possible.

In case you have not realized it; I have not written this next sentence in my 100+ entries. We all could have died that day. A slightly different angle, if we went off the road into the trees, if another car was in the road. Any variation could have had a much more horrific outcome.

Which brings me to my response. Humor, albeit sometimes dark, has gotten me through these tough times. But my answer also reflects the two people I am now. Strong and independent Ironman me, and weak and needing assistance "please pick up the 100th thing I dropped today" me. I strive to be the first. Quick wit, humorous answers, badass survivor. But the second me, the one I initially hated, is growing on me. As I struggle with sleep tonight, I think I have to let the second me out more. My answers don't have to be what I think people expect from me. Admitting things are hard or days are bad, or I had a setback, or a rough day is ok.

"This has to be the worst thing ever that happened to you."

It is most certainly in the top three.

CLOSE, BUT NO CIGAR

PT went well yesterday. I will only have one more session. I walked with a cane to the neighbor's house and with a few stops back. What did we learn? I am still not ready for the cane.

We had a very honest conversation. While I was ahead of all of the milestones, the swelling coupled with these muscles not working properly is stopping me from walking unencumbered. There was hope but given the extent of my injuries and surgeries I am just not ready. So, what then I asked?

Time to get a rollator walker (4 wheels and brakes). This will help normalize my gait but still give me enough support. It will be anywhere from 2 weeks to 2 months. After that? Pretty sure I will need a cane long term.

A few months ago that would have seemed wonderful. Now? A bit of a disappointment. I was hoping for more. For now. I am so close I can taste it. It was a big letdown. A letdown like all other sucky news I have no choice to deal with.

Off to the surgeon this am. Got to see my new X-rays. WOW! Had the bandage removed- all good. Now for the barrage of questions. Swelling, position of my foot (points out), pain in my knee, pins and needles, medications, etc. etc. etc. I was prepared.

We cover everything. Then he repeats what the PT said. Technically the hip is fine, he walks through every X-ray, every step of the surgery. Then he looks at me – straight in the eyes – pauses and says, "You have had a major injury, and 2 major surgeries. It has been months, while you have been working the muscles, they are tight and still not working to walk." He too had hoped for better, but is thrilled by the outcome, by me telling him of daily progress. He said one day I would look down and everything would just be good, and I would not have even noticed. He too said 2 weeks, 2 months, I will know when it's time. He also said yes plan on a cane long term.

He gave me a cortisone shot to try and kickstart the process. Will be tough the next few days. I can go back into the office starting Monday. He told me by the next checkup things will be so much better. I believe him.

I looked at him and paused. "Thank you for giving me hope. Thank you for giving me back my life."

I had to go and test out walkers. I am now the proud owner of a badass gold rollator. Yup, gold. The sales lady was so excited for the new color they got. Initially I was thinking Ironman red, but in Florida wheelchairs and walkers are prevalent. Red is popular. Ironman's other color is gold, so gold it is. It also has brakes, a seat, and a storage compartment.

Today I am resting. Tomorrow, I start again. Two weeks, two months…it's just a matter of time.

REALITY IS SETTING IN

Using my new golden chariot is testing the only upper body muscles I have not yet trained. I passed my last PT session. I can safely get in and out of the house by myself with the new walker. Cut a few minutes off my initial time off the walk to the neighbors. Went up the stairs with a cane – just to prove I can, this is not something I plan on doing for a while. I am most certainly not going to miss walking with someone yanking on the back of my pants.

The cortisone shot is not helping. My knee is not cooperating. My gait is not smooth. I still have high hopes but am now being more realistic. The doctor said I would walk but was not sure how. Now I understand. The limp, the need for an assisted device be it a walker or a cane, this was always a possibility. Actually, it was more a probability. Yet I keep pushing, trying, hoping. Maybe, just maybe, I can still do a little better. I take walks throughout the day, small walks, but still. They exhaust me.

There are still wins. I put a pillow between my knees and rolled on my side. Finally! I was able to be in a position other than flat on my back. I can only handle a few minutes, but it's a start. I have been lowering the height of the commode a little at a time. A few more days or a week and I think I can banish that along with the crutches, old walker, and wheelchair. It's the little things, like being able to get off of a toilet without needing arm supports that I look forward to. Also wearing regular underwear. Due to the swelling, I am still in granny panties as they are easier to get on and don't aggravate the incisions.

I can't wait to be able to do more things. I try and shave my legs by jerry-rigging a razor to my shower stick. I don't see myself getting rid of the shower bench soon either. It would be nice to be able to walk in and out of a shower. I still can't cut my own toenails. I think the sock aid will be my friend for a long while. I wonder if there will be a day I can carry a cup of coffee to the table.

My patio is my favorite spot in my house. I enjoy sitting outside with a drink and enjoying the view of my little lake. I can't get out to the patio on my own. I have only been able to sit outside 2x since I have been home. John is doing everything – it seems to be too much of an imposition to have him help me in and out when he gets home, makes dinner, does the dishes, takes care of the dog, etc. etc. etc. Next goal – patio

WALKING WALKING WALKING

Today I went for my longest walk.

I went past the neighbor's and back and added next door before I returned home. I am going to put these wheels to the test. I am also putting me to the test. After my little jaunt I needed to rest. I came back sweating and exhausted. But I left the house on my own two feet (with the golden chariot) and returned the same way. John thinks I am going too fast. I am still struggling with having to make multiple stops along the way. I need to build stamina. I need to build strength. Right now, my recovery is still zapping my energy.

My very photogenic friend will be in Florida soon for a mini vacation. We will hook up for lunch at a minimum. I can't wait to see her – it's amazing how much I miss everyone. Unfortunately, I have not been a great friend as I am so tired and tend to rest by 5ish so I can get up and eat dinner with the family then be in bed at a ridiculously early time. She and I spoke the other day about how the BOOM brought us closer. It did.

I can't wait to walk to her. I want to have improved my gait by the time I see her. I want to be able to show her the fruit of the months of her and everyone else's support. I still want so much.

I'VE HIT A WALL

Walking is not getting easier. Sometimes during the day, I can speed up the pace, but it's still grueling. I also feel like I pulled something, but I can't tell if it's just the increase in swelling. I don't remember doing anything that may have caused this. Pins and needles set in everyday at 5 like clockwork. I am drained after going small distances.

But I'm still walking, and waiting for the muscles to remember, and losing patience. I keep hoping the day is near where I can just walk.

The only way to learn to walk again is to try and walk. Quite a Catch 22. I can't get a good ratio of walking enough without overdoing it.

I've been physically back in the office this week, sitting in my old chair. Another inch closer to normal. It's not a great week due to circumstances not related to the BOOM. Can a distraction at work have led me to a misstep? Is my emotional health affecting my physical health? I am taking a muscle relaxer and a pain killer to try to rest. Hours later there is no change. I scour the internet looking for a way to literally take the next step.

Nothing.

I am torn between wanting to stay in bed for days or returning to my team.

EVERYBODY'S GOING THROUGH SOMETHING

This is my story of coming back from the BOOM. This story is always there with me – it's difficult to ignore a wheelchair or crutches or a walker. I have one speed – slow, so it's not even like I can sneak past you. But I am not the only one dealing with heavy issues.

A friend has stated to me she compares others day to day petty problems to what I am living. "In comparison…"

In comparison, this BOOM has put a lot of things in perspective for me. In comparison I don't sweat the small stuff anymore. But I also don't put the BOOM in comparison to what others are also going through. Yet I have come to realize I have let the BOOM get in the way.

Recently someone I know was involved in their own BOOM – trauma hospital, rehab, and all. Thankfully for not as long and she will be ok. As I read what had happened to her, I didn't realize I was holding my breath. Victim of a careless driver. I was envisioning myself in her situation. I didn't reach out right away because all I could think is how much it sucked. I knew there were no words at that time that would have made any difference, but I should have reached out anyway. I made the mistake of letting the feelings of my BOOM get in the way. Eventually I instant messaged her, so she knew I was thinking of her. I followed her progress online. In another IM, she didn't want to put her BOOM in the same category as mine. I told her it is not a competition, and I truly mean that. Bad things happen, and it does suck. I wish she was never in the situation she finds herself now, and I send positive energy for a full recovery. We are members of the same club. She too is badass and will do well.

Unrelated, another two friends recently lost their fathers. I can't tell you how often I think of them, but like a toddler I nap whenever I can, and find it is generally too late to call when I am up as I usually find myself awake after midnight. The recovery from surgery is again sucking the life out of me, I am exhausted all of the time. The BOOM is in the way again. Anyone who has ever lost a loved one knows how they are feeling right now. All I can do is keep them and their families in my prayers and wait until we meet again to give them each a big hug full of love.

Another friend just lost her father-in-law. She needs to be strong for her family for whom this loss is great. It's tough when your job is to be the strong one. She shoulders this responsibility without thinking. I wish there was something I could do as she has been there for me so many times. But right now, I can just care for my basic needs and am at the mercy of those who drive me place to place. Texting will have to suffice.

The list goes on. I know others are broken right now, for a host of reasons. Having – living – that feeling is overwhelming. All I can offer are words for now of what I have learned from the BOOM…

Life is hard, and many times seems unfair. Make your story one of strength and resilience. Don't let the idea that the universe is out to get you win – don't give it any power. If you let yourself feel powerless you become powerless.

I read somewhere that pain is unavoidable, but suffering is optional. Sometimes you have to let go of what you wanted so you can get what you need. We don't always get to see the bigger picture. Have faith.

Take the time to take stock of the good things in your life, the things you are grateful for. It's hard to be angry and grateful at the same time.

As for me, I'm going to work harder at not letting the BOOM get in the way.

I'M FRUSTRATED THAT I'M FRUSTRATED AND FRUSTRATED AT MYSELF

Meg-leg has been sore. I think it's making me cranky. Walking is the same, which means no better. I have gotten used to seeing some progress no matter how small, so this no progress is making me crazy. It's frustrating.

Then I think back 5 months ago when walking of any kind was a dream. I didn't care if I needed a walker, but now? Now I do. I feel I can do better. I see myself walking, to the point I have gotten up and started to take a step before I realized I still can't walk unaided. Then I am frustrated again.

I sat outside work the other day waiting on John to pick me up. This walker has a seat for when I can no longer stand safely. Hard to miss me sitting in the golden chariot. A coworker whom I have not seen walked up to me, hand on my shoulder inquiring about my progress. Slow and steady is my reply, with a hope for a brighter future. But there was something in how he looked that let me ask about him. His story is not mine to tell, but one I never hope to find myself in. I lost myself as I couldn't help but envision changing places – and I shuddered as I thought, there but for the grace of God go I.

And frustration abounded. How dare I continue to let this feeling of frustration keep creeping in each day? The thankful feeling fades as the frustration takes the lead. How do I make it stop? I need to finish strong, not go gently into the night. I need to take the positives and let them drive me rather than have these small pity parties. There but for the grace of God.

So today I tried harder. My friend came to my job to have lunch, taking time out of a much-needed vacation to Uber her way to me. I've been bringing lunch and eating in my office because it's easier, but not today. I ordered in from my favorite local restaurant and got myself to the lobby to wait for her.

My team worries if I'm not in my office, so like a 5-year-old I have to let them know where I'll be and for how long as well as take my phone. I told them of my dear friend, who was a gift to me when I was in rehab, who was one of the ones who saved me.

The human contact when most of my loved ones were so far away brought me comfort. She never flinched, she never paused, she never gave up on me. We had nights of pizza and burgers and movies on my iPad. We had laughs and we had quiet. There were times her visits were the only thing that kept me from beating my head against a wall and screaming. Her visits brought normal to my hell. They were different than LLBFF's visits – LLBFF was in the car, the ambulance, the hospital. The memories we share of this BOOM and the aftermath are ours alone. This friend took on a role of helping pick up the pieces that is me without being part of the BOOM.

I stood when I saw her, and we both smiled as we hugged. I'm in much better condition than when she saw me last. I would have taken her upstairs to my office while we waited on the delivery, but I know my limitations. The trips up and down would be too much. We caught up in an empty room, and then moved to the cafeteria to enjoy our lunch. We chatted some more before she left. It felt good to be able to walk beside my friend. Such a simple thing.

I finished the day but am super sore. I've been in bed since I've gotten home. Went through my ice pack. But for today at least, I am not frustrated. Today I had lunch with my friend. Today I had normal.

I guess that's how it will be – the ups and downs. The frustration and the normal. All I know is I will continue working so that hopefully by the next time I see her I will be without the golden chariot.

NORMAL

Last night I needed a painkiller. It was rough. Tonight, I had an extremely normal night.

My friend's sister was coming into town, (she is a long-distance friend of mine). We "planned" to catch up. I rested earlier in the day – knowing my limits if I was to try and venture out. Everything zaps my strength. At one point I placed a pillow between my knees and moved slightly to my side.

I fell asleep. Sleeping on my side.

When I got up, I showered and changed in a new record of 40 minutes. We headed to our friend's home where I took the golden chariot across her front lawn. I specifically got a walker with larger wheels to accommodate the potential of being on Florida grass. Success. We spent time in her living room until we headed out to dinner. Wonderful Thai meal and a lot of fun. We went back to her house for coffee and conversation. It was easy, it was normal. I spoke about the BOOM and the aftermath many times during the night, sometimes with laughter, sometimes with sorrow. I spoke of my frustration, of being stuck at this plateau of progress.

John made mention of checking on me and seeing me asleep on my side. He didn't remember when he last saw that. My friend stated she did not expect to see me this well all things considered. Everyone agrees I am so far along, have made so much progress. And I need to be patient. ***sigh***

I did make an egg on a toasted bagel today all by myself. Another step closer.

I LIED AND LAUGHED AND LAUGHED

Over five months since the BOOM and almost everyday someone asks me what happened. The other day I just out and out lied. Said it was an Alpine skiing accident. Zigged when I should have zagged. Should have seen the look on the other persons face, and then I broke out in laughter.

I think I'm going to continue doing that. Just giving absurd answers.

- Killer volleyball game
- Extreme game of chicken – I won
- Frogger (in real life) – I lost
- Rock climbing accident

- In a buffalo stampede

- Roller derby tryouts

- Ice fishing accident

- Shark attack

- Got hit with a paralyzing blow dart

- Tried to hit a Caballerial on my board but tanked it

- Mountain lion attack

- Bar fight

Still with the golden chariot. I continue to try using a cane at home. I also continue to realize I am not ready for a cane. In a few days it will be 6 weeks since the 2nd surgery and I still cannot walk without a walker. 164 days and counting since I was able to walk unaided. I will be seeing the surgeon this week. I am going to ask for an X-ray as I have some discomfort which makes me nervous. Fingers crossed.

Today I had to re-lace my right sneaker. The swelling is still present from my hip to my ankle, but the swelling in my foot is gone. I still have to use the kindergarten elastic laces, but I am not skipping holes. I am still living in the guest room but have been doing my own laundry for 2 weeks now. It took 10 minutes, and I was dripping sweat, but I was able to trim my own toenails today. I have to look for progress wherever I can to prove to myself the BOOM is not winning. I have to take a win no matter how small. Even though everything I do still zaps my strength I have to keep going, keep fighting. Still continuing on my journey to that single step

MY REALITY

I stare at a picture of my x-rays, showing so much that no one can see. This is my reality. This is what I have been looking at the last few days – to remind myself – to visualize – why I am still not where I want to be.

I went for my next follow up with the surgeon. I have been very nervous. I'm not in pain, but a high level of discomfort. Initially I thought it was just muscular, the walking is taking its toll. Then as I thought of the last time I felt like this, it turned out I had a broken bone on my ass tablet and a collapsed femoral head. I was getting around with broken bones and naively agreed it must just be muscular.

It's tough with the cane so I stayed with the walker until the Dr. could do some X-rays. No sense in chancing going backwards. My youngest drove Ms. Daisy this time, and on the way to the Dr. I was texting with a friend. I needed to calm my nerves. "It will be fine." I could only hope.

When I arrived, the nurse asked how I was doing and I told her about the discomfort and asked if I were getting X-rays, because if I wasn't scheduled I needed one. I was, so the tech took me, and I got a new set of pictures. The doctor's assistant then came in, apparently the nurse told her I wasn't 100%. She wanted to know what was going on and why I thought something happened. Brought her up to speed on how my mind is working these days. "You are fine," she stated. Not flippantly, not as a knee jerk response, but she said it as she looked at me reassuringly. She said the films are good, and started to explain, again, how I am not the average patient. She was briefing me when the doctor came in.

He looked, paused, and smiled. "This looks great" – I wonder how we can look at the same pictures and have two very diverse thoughts. His clinical eye brings me comfort. We go through everything again. The discomfort is mainly being felt now as nerves are regenerating. That too is causing the spasms. Also, the bones are knitting into the hardware. All of that, plus walking, is pulling these muscles which have still not adapted to having my leg lengthened. Time. All I need is time. We talk talk again about how long this can truly take to heal. ***sigh***. I am both comforted and saddened by the news; nothing is wrong, but my body is still fighting me to recover from the BOOM.

I will continue to have discomfort and spasms. I will continue to have this never-ending fatigue. He tells me how hard my body is working to welcome the many new pieces. He tells me as I start to use the cane more in the house I will have this feeling in other muscles, every different movement walking uses a new set. He said I will know when the golden chariot can be retired and not to rush it. The cane is close. He tells me so much that I already know – I was in a serious accident and had two major surgeries. New day, same song.

I look at this picture, because in my mind, in my dreams, and sometimes when I just stand, I can walk. Until I am faced with the reality of no I can't. It doesn't sadden me as much as it grounds me. It takes the words I hear from everyone–

"You were in a serious accident and had two major surgeries," - and makes me reassess where I am. It's a tangible reminder. Ironman had a lot of pieces parts too.

172 DAYS OR 24 WEEKS AND 4 DAYS

My youngest was home for Spring Break which means we saw him sparingly. Last night we planned a family dinner out before he had to go back to school, all four of us and just a normal night out.

Earlier in the week he drove me to the doctor. For those that don't know, I have two big boys who drive trucks. He had asked me if I could get into his truck, a feat that even a week ago was daunting. "Let's see" was my answer. I still needed a step to step up, but was able to get in. No longer tied to my ride, if I could get in that truck, I could get into anything.

So emboldened by that trip, each day since the doctor I have tried using the cane a little more in the house. It is tough and like everything else tiring. Last night John asked me if I wanted to try the cane for our outing. "Let's see."

I walked slowly, even more slowly than what is my new normal, out the door and into his truck (with help). He drove straight up to the door of the restaurant. I walked in and as luck would have it, all the way to the back where we were seated. We had a great dinner, and a bunch of laughs. Reverse and back in the truck and into the house. That was more than enough for me.

It has taken 172 days or 24 weeks and 4 days since I was able to go anywhere not in a wheelchair or on crutches or with a walker. I still can't go anywhere on my own.

Today I needed the walker again but yesterday gave me a glimpse of what my next phase will be. I have been looking at canes for a while now. There are so many that are badass. But as I felt the callousness in my hand, I made a decision that did not take my vanity into account. I ordered a carbon fiber adjustable cane with a derby handle. It is super light, super strong and at least black with a cool pattern. My current collapsible cane will be the backup. For now, it is my training cane to get me through the next step.

THIS WEEKS MILESTONES BROUGHT TO YOU BY…

The letter C for Cane, L for Lunch, and T for toilet.

My new cane came in the mail. It is carbon fiber and super super light. I also ordered a strap so if I need to use my hand for anything not walking related the cane will not fall to the floor – like almost everything else does. I brought it to work mid-week, still using the golden chariot to get in from the parking lot. For my morning and afternoon strolls around the office and to go to about half of the meetings I used the cane. After the first day, I turned my alarm off the next morning and went back to sleep. Using the cane now had me break my current record time of getting ready in the am – 32 minutes. Of course, I did not have breakfast or coffee at home, or pack a lunch, and I will admit my teeth brushing was probably not optimal.

Walking is hard.

I am pretty fast most days with the walker. I say pretty fast just as a comparison to how I've been getting around lately. But I still am rocky each time I get up and need to get my bearings and stretch. One hand is significantly more calloused than the other, this is a testament to how much I still need to lean on the handles of the walker. I still need to stop, shake it out, and rest when using the walker.

Walking with the cane? Back several months in my speed and stability. But like everything associated with the BOOM, I have to practice, practice, practice. I don't do anything well to begin with. But I deal with the fatigue which is now exasperated – by my body still trying to grow bones and heal, and the different workout using a cane. Yet it is amazing that I am standing. Milestone – cane.

Bonus to using a cane? I can get out on the patio by myself. My favorite spot in my house. I can feel the warm breeze, hear the birds, listen to the sound of the waterfall from the pool. Florida living at its best. It's taken 5 1/2 months for me to be able to get out my back door. FIVE AND A HALF MONTHS. Patience is not my virtue.

I let the dog out in the yard this week. I had to navigate the patio slider, the screen door, and the gate. Reverse, repeat. I explained to the dog I understood this to be an emergency for him, no one else was home, but we need to go slow and be careful. Cujo actually listened. But now he thinks we can do it all the time. Nay nay puppy. This is a special event, kind of like going out for ice cream.

I also got an unexpected text this week, a menu from an awesome Mexican dive restaurant by work, and an invitation for lunch. You don't realize how your world changes when you can't drive. The appreciation of people coming to me is another thing that is hard to articulate. While we had a great meal, and discussed the BOOM, we also spoke about planning to go to the movies. The last movie I saw in a theater? The Meg last summer (maybe that's why I can't help the nickname for my leg). The conversation is the milestone – letting me bring normal talks back into my life. An inane discussion about going to a movie. Normal.

My life remains full of adaptive tools. Grabbers, 3-foot shoehorn, dressing stick, bed rails, etc, etc, etc. They are in my bed, my office, and around the house. But they do not affect anyone else. Larger items are being banished to the garage as I longer no require them; extra wheelchair, crutches, walker #1, etc, etc, etc. My home will eventually be a museum to the BOOM.

So as I went to use the restroom, I looked at the commode. It sits above our toilet, so I have handles on either side. When I am out I of course use handicapped restrooms. The height of the toilets in addition to the handrails let me be safe. I refused to install grab bars in our home. Drilling through the tiles and the walls would always be a permanent reminder. I opted for the commode and a shower bench. Since the second surgery I have been able to lower the height several times.

So I stood and stared. I sized up one of my last enemies that is a reminder to my family and to my guests. Anytime anyone has to use the restroom they are faced with the fact that I still am struggling with a handicap. I could lower it one more time, or I could go big or go home. So like with everything that I need to try, I did a test run. I moved it to the shower, made sure I had my cell phone in my pocket in case things went south, and tried to sit. Slow, a bit unsteady, but doable. Up? I was scared to try. I sat fully dressed sitting on a toilet for a few minutes rethinking my stupidity of not waiting for John to do this. My friend has given me the term helicopter husband. He worries about every move still. If he were there, he would tell me wait. It doesn't matter. It's not a big deal. Yet it is to me. Everything matters. So up I stood.

I stood.

Boo-ya!! Milestone: I can pee where I want to. This takes away the need to plan. How much can I drink, where will I be, can I use the facilities safely? It no longer limits where I can go. These are things that unfortunately have become part of my life for the past 178 days. And yes I am still counting. I still count and measure everything. I am still counting for that first step.

This does not mean that I am getting rid of the commode just yet. I understand it is stupid to struggle when there is no need or can have adverse effects. But what it did let me know was that if I wanted to visit a friend, I could have a drink and not worry about having to use their bathroom, not an ideal situation, but life changing in a pinch.

YESTERDAY WAS MY SEMI-CRASHIVERSARY

Is this something to celebrate? Should I have had cake?

It's been six months since the BOOM. S I X M O N T H S

Six months of trials and tribulations. Six months since my life, and those close to me, has been altered. Six months and I still need a walker.

I have been doing a lot of reading about/by car crash survivors, although I still haven't encountered another broken ass tablet. Basically, it sucks. I'm impatient counting months (really, mostly days). Others are counting years. I hope to be walking soon but have resigned myself a cane will be my long-term friend, perhaps for life. A friend that continually sucks the life out of me but still needed, I think we all have one of those.

If I have to hang something on a wall, I usually end up with more holes than I needed. Sometimes I use multiple nails because it just doesn't look like it will hold. When I look at my X-rays, I still don't get how I stay together with all the screws +++++, yet it does hold.

But…

The fatigue…, the not driving, the not walking unaided. Did I mention the fatigue? I'm done, I just need to rest, to take shelter from this storm. How do you get through it? How do you keep fighting through the days, like yesterday where the weather had me take two (figurative) steps back? Then I remember something I read on one of the crash sites; I'm not a victim, I'm a survivor. You choose which one you want to be.

Six months in and still counting.

WE GOT A NEW DOG

We have always had pets – note the plural. Dogs, snakes, ferrets, fish, mice, the list goes on. The week of the BOOM we had to put down my dog. His health had seriously declined, and it was no longer fair to him, it was just hard for us. I didn't have time to truly mourn as I was heading to NY. While I was in rehab, I got a call that his ashes were ready, the place we had him euthanized will arrange for a cremation and an interment in a pet columbarium. I owed him so much this was the least I could do to repay him. I explained my situation on the phone and asked them to take care of him for me, as I had no idea when I would be able to. Just add this to the list of things I couldn't do.

Obviously, with everything going on there was no way to bring a new pet into the mix. Our dog, actually my husband's dog, would just have to go it on his own for a bit. It would be the first time in his life he was an only pet.

I started to look into service dogs when in rehab. They cost anywhere from $15-50k. So, ok, I wouldn't be getting a service dog. However, I did some research, and I could have a dog (one that we have) trained to do just the tasks I would need at a much more reasonable cost. Ok, I would wait and see how my life turned out.

John went into puppy mode, researching and scouring the internet. We would not get a pup until I could safely navigate the house. Our estimate would be hopefully by the summer. Our youngest would-be home from school to help out.

Then one evening I was resting my ass tablet, John comes into the guest room to show me a picture and video of a dog that is the spitting image of the one we have, another all-black German shepherd. A friend of his sent him the info, the dog needed a home. He is two years old and housebroken. But he was living with a bit older of a couple in a condo. He needed a house and he needed someone to play with. I will say this couple tried everything to make it work, extensive dog training, doggy day care, but he was just a bit too much for them to handle.

So we inquired, went through numerous calls, more questions than I thought we would get trying to adopt a child. He has the same food allergies as our dog which makes things easier. A meet and greet with our dog to make sure they get along. He was even trained to do the stairs with the couple. Should I eventually need that, we would bring him back to the trainer to solidify that task for me. Pictures were sent to his owners with all of our information. We agreed to take him, and they agreed we would be a good family.

John picked him up while I was working. Just like a new baby I was getting pictures and updates.

This guy, while well-loved has had his share of issues. He is now @75 pounds and will probably fill out to 90-95. He lived with a couple in an apartment and was shuttled to day care before he was surrendered to the trainer to try and find him a good family. He lived for a few weeks at their training/boarding facility. And now he is with us. New home, new environment, new noises, and no one he knows. Boy, can I relate.

When I came home, he was barking and John had to hold him back. He is already protecting his home, I guess he forgot me from our visit. He had a good start, hanging with the boys and Cujo. Got to play outside, inside and hang on the patio watching the birds. He instantly found the basket of toys Cujo had long abandoned and took out every single toy and has them all over the house. As well trained as he is, he is not quite listening yet as you can tell he is a bit overwhelmed.

As for me? The last few days have been rough, the rainy weather is killing my ass tablet, causing some pain. The pain is giving me a headache, which led to an upset stomach. I was ready for bed.

In the middle of the night, I was awoken, and it took me a few minutes to get my bearing. There was Radar crying loudly at the side of my bed. I slowly sat up and called him over. He needed some love and reassurance. I talked smoothly to him as I pet his head and told him how scary my first night in rehab was. I told him I understand that being in a new place at night by yourself is tough. I told him "You will be fine."

At that point the other dog came in and nudged him a bit before he sat next to him. He did venture upstairs but ended up back with me. He was in and out all night so we both had a long night. When I got up a few hours later to use the rest room, he was asleep outside my door.

He will be ok; he has his crew.

A HAIRCUT AND A PRAYER

I've mentioned before how anesthesia and meds really f' with your hair, scalp, skin, stomach, (I think you can follow along). I've been letting my hair grow out so I could get all the "dead" removed. In the meantime, I did one hot oil treatment that was wonderful but not quite effective enough.

As I still rely on people to drive Ms. Daisy it's not easy to make a hair appointment, especially when you live with men who in a pinch will just use the clippers they have and do a buzz cut. I tried to make an appointment the other week, but they were booked. Then I didn't have the number with me. I gave up and decided to just go to one of those walk-in places. Ironic huh, a walk-in place. I'm so over not being able to go and do things when and where I want.

John took me today, dropped me off in front with my cane, and went to park the car. Like every dutiful husband, he sat on a bench outside to wait for me.

Limp, limp, limp in I went. I told the stylist I needed a good shampoo and deep conditioning in addition to a haircut. Off we went, and of course I could see she wanted to ask what happened. I gave the abridged version, (which I now excel at) and brought it back to hair and scalp. Anesthesia and meds, what could she recommend trying and start to fix this?

She recommended several products, and we agreed on a course of action. Then I had one of the best shampoos in my life. The massage was relaxing, the product smelled sweet and calming. I wasn't really listening to her chatter but then noticed she paused, which got my attention. I apologized and asked her what she said.

She hesitated and asked if I believed in God.

I replied, "Yes. How could I not after what I have been through?"

She stated I am not alone during my recovery and while this is tough, Jesus too had suffered. God walks with me now. I joked, but a bit slowly these days. We then went back to general chatter.

Fast forward to the finish of my cut as she was "swooshing" my hair, then she laid her hands upon me and stated, "I pray to God that He heals you, and that you find your purpose in this accident. Because it happened for a reason."

Not the outing I was expecting. As I struggle with my walking, or lack thereof, was there a reason I popped into that salon today? When I have these moments of frustration and pity something or someone eventually happens in my day to help put things back in perspective.

I am home, sitting on the patio in the shade of a beautiful Florida afternoon. I go on the patio whenever I want now, all by myself. Well, not exactly today…

I sit with Zeus (aka Cujo) and Radar. They are enjoying the gentle breeze and sounds of the birds with me.

THOUGHTS OF MY GRANDMOTHER AS I TOOK A STEP

My grandmother was born in Sicily. While I don't know the exact particulars, I do know she had an accident where she fell and broke both of her legs. Health care being what it was there and then, her legs never healed "back to normal". Her height was stunted, and her legs somewhat bowed. All of my memories of my grandmother include her and her cane. She would go slow and carefully, with a little waddle as she walked unevenly.

I've been using the cane, but it eludes me except for short bouts. But yet I try. While in the house I used the cane to get over to the couch. When I later got up, the cane had moved to the side of the end table. I stood, and then took a tentative step. And then another as I braced myself on the couch. I lurched and waddled a few feet, and it seemed familiar. Then I remembered my grandmother. My few steps mirrored hers. I never realized…

I never realized how hard it was for her. I never realized how draining walking must have been. I never realized how hard it would have been for her to come to America. I never realized she did not play and chase me as child – because she couldn't. My grandfather and father were the ones who would be outside with me, not agreeing on the use of training wheels for my bike (for the record; one would put them on, the other take them off). Summers in the Catskills, but she never once came. How much did we miss together because she just couldn't? I don't know, I'll never know. I am saddened by how much I did not realize.

My cousin had posted a picture of the matriarchs of our family on Facebook some time ago, captioned by…

A few of the strong women I come from

My grandmother is in the middle. This has become one of my favorite pictures. There could be no better words than what my cousin used to describe this photo. My mother and sister are directly to the right of my grandmother. With the exception of one great Aunt, I grew up with all of these women pictured who were my inspiration and role models. They defined strength.

I surmise this is why I can continue on, I come from strong women. I will take the benefit of great surgeons, technology, advances in medicine, things never afforded to my grandmother, and I will walk.

But for tonight? Tonight, I will smile as I remember Grandma, and hope she is looking down smiling as I toddle along for a few steps at a time. I hope she thinks I am a strong woman too.

I'M A CYBERNETIC ORGANISM. LIVING TISSUE OVER A METAL ENDOSKELETON

It's Groundhog Day in April. Another visit to the surgeon. Park, elevator, waiting room, exam room, x-ray, and wait. Repeat every 4-6 weeks.

I should be more thrilled that everything looks good, that my transformation into a terminator is progressing. The bone continues to grow into and around and through the prosthesis and plates and screws. Yet still I am frustrated. Every day is now pretty much like the day before, no great improvement. I need independence.

John took my car away from me, literally. Like everything I do, I must devise a MacGyver way to do it and then practice. I drive an SUV, or I did. I can't get into the driver's seat because it is too high. I need to practice getting in safely as a first step to driving. I scoured the internet, watched videos, checked the crash support group. The only way to do it is to use a step (which we have) and tie a rope (which I don't have) to it and pull it in once you are inside the vehicle. That's where my mistake was made. I asked John for some rope.

I might as well have asked for a brick of C4. He adamantly states I was not driving (reminder, I was not driving when the BOOM happened and am a passenger in a car almost daily, but I digress). I told him I wasn't driving; I need to practice getting in. Nope, so he took my keys and drives my car so it's not on the driveway for me to access.

John takes me to my latest and greatest checkup. He feels the need to speak on my behalf – I'm sure you can guess how I felt about that, so I'll keep this G rated and decline to comment further. He tells the doctor I am frustrated. That- wait for it –

I was in a serious accident and had two major surgeries.

Insert giant face palm now.

I acknowledge the frustration. The doctor reminds me how great it is that I have come so far. I go in for the kill as I am 87% sure based on previous conversations, I know what his response will be. Let's talk driving.

John mutters under his breath "like that's going to happen."

The doctor pauses and states I need to practice getting in and out of the car safely. Practice stepping on the brake. Then he tells John when I can do that, he should take me driving in a store parking lot on a Sunday afternoon. I won't be driving on I-95, but this needs to start somewhere. An increase in independence is what I need to lower the frustration. I cheer a bit and tell the doc he took my car away. Game, set, match.

I will be back in another 6 weeks. As I stand the doctor comments, he wishes he videotaped my progress. That 6 weeks ago I was not able to stand so quickly and so well. I tell him it depends on the day.

As John drives me to work, he states he is worried. I get it now, the thought of anything happening again is paralyzing. I know that feeling too well when things are out of your control. What he doesn't get is I need to get some of that control back. I understand, I sympathize, and I empathize. But I still need to try.

So when do you keep trying vs. giving up? I am about to quit the crash survivor's support group. We are a mixed group of people – from fender benders to roll overs with injuries ranging from scratches to PTSD to TBIs. Most of our stories have some common thread. But these are not my people. Many are broken in spirit, seeing no way out of where they are. They are resigning themselves to a certain life or lack thereof. While I have my days, I cannot let that be my life. I am not judging. If things were more severe, if I did not have the support I do, if – if – if. I could go on. You can't decide what other people choose to do, you can only be there and support their decisions. You can't know until you walk a mile in their shoes. It's easy to say what you would do; it is very different when you have to live it.

As for me, I keep going. Later today I will practice getting in my vehicle. I will most certainly fail. Time and time again I will fail. I will be frustrated. Then I will try again another day. For me, I continue to fight for the *possibility.*

MAJOR MILESTONE

I got in MY CAR today. Without a step. In the driver's seat. Multiple times.

I failed time and time again, doing it the way I was instructed. Then I stepped back. I have been evolving in how I live my life. There are so many things I do differently than before the BOOM. Maybe, just maybe, I needed to not follow convention.

So only with my cane I stood before the running board. I needed to grab the bad leg to help lift it high enough. I pivoted and was able to get in the seat by the power of the non-BOOM side. Slight adjustment to the seat position. I was in. But once was not enough.

Out of the car, repeat. Out again, repeat.

I sat and smiled. This is the first step to some independence. If I could I would have jumped in the air. It has been over 200 days since I was behind the wheel, even if the car wasn't even on.

Next step was to see if I could push down on the brakes, move to the gas, back to the brakes. Repeat. Repeat. Repeat. Success!

Out in the driveway I went. John was coming back from getting the mail. I told him I could do it. Do what I could not just a few short weeks ago. He paused, and then wanted to see for himself. I was confident-success again. This was enough for today.

Next week we will practice driving in an empty parking lot. As ready as I am is how not ready he is. He would wrap me in bubble wrap and keep me in the house if at all possible.

I need to figure how best to get the walker in my SUV on my own. I still need it. I can't do the cane for more than short jaunts of time and distance. I am planning.

I ordered a raincoat. I won't be able to get in and out while holding an umbrella. I am planning.

I am thinking of where I will go first on my own, somewhere close to home, somewhere I can manage alone. I am planning.

Finally, I am planning again. Today is a good day.

220 DAYS

It's been 220 days since I last drove my car.

220 DAYS.

Well, that streak is now…

Shattered – like I have been. I wish there were some kind of sound effect that could have played as I drove. Something to mark this momentous occasion. Something to show the BOOM it's my bitch now.

I drove today. First just around a small parking lot to make sure I could hit the brakes.

Then around my community.

Then in the real world.

Granted its late afternoon on Easter Sunday and everyone is most likely eating. But I was on the road.

I can get in and out of the car – not easily but I can do it. I can put my walker in the way back and get it out. Again – not easily but I can do it. I can do it – I can drive.

The seatbelt rubs on my surgical site, I need a small towel to protect my ass tablet. I need to physically lift my BOOM leg up to the running board. Small price to pay.

I can gain back some of my lost independence. I can get a cup of coffee on the way to work. I am no longer a prisoner. I can come and go as I please.

Of course, rainy days will be nearly impossible. Driving on the highway is not going to be anytime soon. Long trips are also not on my short-term plan. But I can go to work, I can go to the pharmacy, I can… just go. I will leave ridiculously early to avoid traffic. But it will be a start.

I may not be walking but this is a big first step.

I once held your hand in the ER

This was a message I got a week ago. In an instant I knew who it was. It was my LLBFF's friend who came to the first hospital the day of the BOOM.

I never thanked her personally. To say I wasn't up for company in rehab is putting it mildly. As time went by, I was focused on my goal of walking and getting out of there. Basic niceties were not on my radar. Yet that does not mean I do not think of what she did often.

It took me half an hour to respond as I framed my reply. I needed to convey what her actions meant to me. Here is my response:

"Believe it or not, it's one of the things I remember fondly. I never got a chance to thank you properly. I was not in a good place while in rehab. I hope LLBFF passed along my thanks. I don't know if your ears ever ring, but I tell people often of your kindness.

In and out from drugs and pain, there were moments where my brain worked but I could not articulate anything. I could hear and remember most everything. When I saw you and you explained holding my hand – that was one of those moments.

All these months later I still get asked about the BOOM (I use a walker so it's kind of obvious something happened). People will ask questions or share with me something about a loved one. I ALWAYS tell them – hold their hand and talk to them. They know. I knew.

Forever grateful for kindness during the darkness."

Two hundred and twenty-eight days later and I still get asked. I have perfected my synopsis in under a minute. Unless… sometimes someone will have specific questions. The majority of people aren't obnoxious in their questioning, rather it seems to me they are looking for some kind of insight. Most of those who question me ask about what I remember about the first days. And so I tell them. This lady is always featured.

I knew of her from conversations through the years – how you learn about your friend's friends. I met her only once. Yet this woman sat with me and held my hand through my terrible ordeal. I remember vividly the calmness in the cadence of her voice.

The kindness of strangers.

I have been reflecting about my response to her this last week. Why after all this time did she message me now?

I've mentioned the crash survivor support group and how I have been leaning towards leaving. So many of them are struggling. So many are giving up the fight. So many are alone in their darkness.

I understand now. They need someone to hold their hand. They need a calming and reassuring voice. They are reaching out and hoping for the kindness of strangers. They need someone to hold their hand across the internet.

Today I went to the movies with my sons. My first movie since last summer. We went to an early show to avoid crowds. Since the BOOM I have not been anywhere I have to walk through crowds. My son drove and I decided to just take my cane. I selected a movie closest to the door, but it was still a daunting task. But I did it. I'm up this late as the muscle in my thigh is reminding me I walked using only the cane. Well, you know what? F' you BOOM! I went to the f'ing movies with my kids!

I continue my fight every day. I am still frustrated; I am exhausted and I am still nowhere closer to where I want to be. But I will fight for normal. I will fight for visiting with friends and driving to work and seeing a movie. I will fight for the little wins I can get.

I will share the story of the woman who held my hand as I will share this day with the crash survivors. It will demonstrate the change in my life in the last 228 days.

A BLUE DAY

Yesterday I got my permanent disabled parking placard. I had a temporary one that could be renewed every six months. Temporary is red, permanent is blue. How ironic that the color also reflected my feelings.

In my head after the second surgery my recovery was temporary – hell I wouldn't even need to renew it again. I have now come to terms I will have a permanent disability – that's does not mean I won't continue to improve, but I am facing reality that the BOOM has lasting effects.

It brought me back to the first days of rehab when I was crashing around in my wheelchair. John continuing to jump to help at my every move. When I told him to stop, I had to learn, adding in my head "to learn to live like this." 234 days after the BOOM the same thought is ringing. Part of learning how to live like this is understanding and accepting my limitations.

It's hard – emotionally and physically. Even when I thought I may be in a wheelchair I had visions of more independence, I would overcome. Reality vs expectations is sometimes a hard pill to swallow.

I am at the point where I can shower in the am before work, but by the time I get ready and pack the walker and my backpack in the car I am dripping with sweat from exertion. It's hard to get in the car. I sit in my driveway for a minute before I can go anywhere. I have not been on a highway yet and frankly have no idea when I will try. I was invited to a birthday lunch with friends during the workweek, something we have been doing for years. Yet I have not responded as I am weighing the extra trip to my car, the drive, and the need to take local streets to get there. Am I up to having to make an extra trip during the day? I still have to nap every day when I get home from work.

Every day I plan, I can't do anything without thinking through the scenarios. Then there are unknown factors – like the weather. This last week we had a number of storms. My ass tablet is sore and swelling. I can't use an umbrella with the walker and have gotten a bit wetter than I would have liked with the rain jacket. There are nights I left everything in the car, to be gotten later by John or one of the boys. It's scary enough getting out of the car and trying to walk on wet ground with a cane. But the OT had prepared me for this scenario. I remember the conversations of me calling him crazy taking me out in bad weather with my walker or crutches, and his response telling me he has to prepare me to live in the real world. It was scary enough back then with one or two people with me to make sure I was ok, it is twice as scary doing it on my own.

So, X-rays and doctor again next week. I am hoping the bones are grafting well enough so I can add some exercises to help with my muscles. I am limited now to only walking as the bone is growing through and around all the metal. I am also hoping the discomfort is due only to the weather. In the mean time…

Hi, my name is Candi and I have a disability. But it does not define me – (spoiler alert- contrary to the Avenger's Endgame – Ironman lives).

238 DAYS – BUT I NEED A MINUTE

Today was a hard day. Another follow up with the surgeon. I had a lot on my mind to discuss; swelling if you even say the word rain, discomfort, and a section of muscle in my leg about 8×6 inches that is prohibiting me from progressing further. It is weak, it is sore, and I can feel it just on the verge of giving out when I try to walk with the cane. The feeling of pins and needles is now gone, sans for my foot when it rains. It is replaced by this annoying small section of good for nothing muscle. Now that I can feel the area again, it stands out to me like a sore thumb.

I did drive myself to the doctor. Bypassing the highway for local streets it took over an hour- my longest drive yet. When I got there the thought of just going in with a cane went bye-bye. I grabbed my walker (easier said than done) and headed up. Same room, same drill. I tell the nurse my woes – she asks I am worse? Compared to what is what I am thinking. I sigh and say no. She states all is expected.

As I wait for the surgeon, I am in the middle of a group text with some friends. It makes me smile. It's hard to explain how little snippets of normal can change your mood, albeit sometimes just a tad. The comments as there are pauses in between as I deal with medical staff have me chuckling.

In comes the doctor, smiling shaking my hand, says hello and states you are frustrated. Well hello to you too. Asks about the muscle, touches it (which hurts). Says to be expected. Some other small talk, then, wait for it….say it with me….

You were in a serious accident and had two major surgeries.

Maybe I should just have that tattooed somewhere so people don't have to keep saying it.

Explains why everything basically sucks but is happy with my progress. Good thing he is cute, or I would beat him with my cane. Oh, forgot it in the car. His lucky day.

He looks me in the eye and says it will be a year from the last surgery until I can walk mostly unaided. I think I should go get the cane after all.

Bone is healing, muscles have been through trauma, moved to and fro with each surgery.

Surely there has to be something I can do to speed this up?

Nope. Nada. Zip. Zilch.

I am crestfallen. NEXT January. We talk about walking with the cane. I broached the subject of an exercise bike with the nurse. I ask him could I possibly add that into my routine?

He agrees- we compromise with the bike if I am not in pain and more cane use. I can not do anything to hurt the muscle, or my setback will be ridiculous. I will be back in July as long as I feel ok.

I get myself back into my car, and I need a minute. 238 days – I am only at 238 days. He is talking 469 Days at best. How do I do it? I need a minute. I can't. I just can't.

I text John. Let him know and head off to work. He knows. He calls immediately.

You were in a serious accident and had two major surgeries.

I can't. I pull into a drive through to get some coffee. A few small tears slip out as he lauds my accomplishments. He is my champion. He knows.

I get myself together. It is not often I have days like this. But when I do – it's ok to take a minute. I head to work already late for a training class. Nothing like rolling in late with the golden chariot. They saved me a seat in the front. Inevitably the instructor asks. Yesterday at a meeting with colleagues from out of town I again used the bar fight answer followed by Frogger in real life. Eventually I give them the real deal. Her today? My 30 second version. She is not getting the best of me.

The rest of the day is hectic, and I get ready to head home later than I would have liked. I am again dripping in sweat as the day took it's toll. I am at my end, and I tell my associate who stops me for a question, I can't. I need to leave. She pauses and asks do I need help to the car. There is no hiding. I thanked her and say no, and head home now in the ever present rain. Stuck in traffic I flip through the channels for some music to lighten the drive. When I get home, I sit in the driveway in the rain. The walker is in the back. ***sigh***

I put on a Yankee cap (always have one handy in the car) and head out. As soon as my foot hits the driveway the door opens – it's John. He knows. He gets my walker and my bag, pausing to give me a kiss hello.

I will be fine; I just need a minute. Or maybe just a night.

99.9% SURE

I am back at the surgeon. I roll my way in, and when they state I don't look to be doing as well as last time. I tell them that is why I'm here.

Back to "my room".

Then x-ray.

Then waiting.

In he comes, positive as always. X-ray looks good. Nothing appears to have moved. Look at the bone.

"Tell my what's going on."

I explain my saga. I finish by saying "I don't say to you I have pain, even though you know how I am doing. I have constant discomfort. Not now. Now, I have pain."

He is 99.9% sure I have hip flexor tendinitis. The tendon is doing more work supplementing the lazy muscle (my medical explain of his technical one). What he says makes sense. It fits. It explains the pain.

So now what?

You get shots for this. A few weeks good as new. Ok, let's do the shot.

Not so fast – of course there is a catch.

He wants to order a CT scan. A particular one that will show shadows with the metal. A test that will let him see everything. He doesn't want to give me the shot if there is any chance something else is wrong.

He is conservative. He is protective.

I am frustrated. I am so over this.

Have the test, come back, we will look at the results (he knows how much I like to see the pictures – it amazes me every time). He will give me the shot then.

"What about the pain?" He acknowledges this is painful. Rx for Percocet.

Off I go.

I WENT IN THE POOL TODAY

It was…. Liberating. I was very shaky and used my cane to get into the water. But as I waded in, I could stand – and I could walk. It took my breath away.

I've read a lot about visualization, seeing yourself actually perform a task or accomplishing something insurmountable. It did not compare to how I felt when I truly saw myself walking unassisted on my own two feet.

There were no jerky movements, no pain. It was freeing unlike anything I have felt in months. I got misty eyed by something so simple. I have hope. I am so tired of hearing just be patient, it will be ok. But today? Today I

SAW, I DID!

John strategically sat on the patio – close in case something went wrong. My forever protector. But he knows how I am now, how I need to strive for independence. He let me do this on my own. He finally called out to see how I was. I enthusiastically shared my wonder.

I will walk again I CAN SEE IT NOW

WHAT WAS I THINKING?

I have now spent the last 2 days in bed recovering from my wonderful pool experience. While I was in the water, I could do anything – I am Ironman after all. When I got out I can only equate to feeling like what the astronauts must have felt like returning to earth – the reality of gravity.

I have tiredness in every cell of my body – it's screaming "What the fuck were you thinking!?"

My leg is killing me. The unused muscles too are letting me know in no uncertain terms don't do that again. My momentary independence has been stripped.

The highs and lows are killing me. I needed a win. Now I am being tortured by my short happiness. I am wearing down. How do I keep going like this? Everyone is sacrificing so much. I try to fit back in, try to live a normal life – but times like these knock me to the ground and my strength is waning.

Tomorrow – tomorrow will be a new day.

WORK IS HARD

I am busy. If I forget to stretch, I can barely move when I try and get up. I need to add 10 minutes to get to meetings. I am exhausted. I am not sleeping well.

I am so busy; I am having pain. I am getting scared.

HOUSTON, WE HAVE A PROBLEM

I got a twinge getting into bed. Not a good twinge, a stop and hold my breath twinge.

I dare not move.

I wait.

I wait some more.

I think, what was I doing? Nothing. I was doing absolutely nothing.

Finally, I move. I am sore. Since the second surgery I say I have discomfort. Everything is to scale based on the pain of the BOOM. Not sure if that is the best gauge, but when they say on a scale of 1-10, 10 being the worst, I am back in that ambulance, I am back screaming so loud that it weakens me after I passed out from the pain. Is that the 10? I have yet to feel good. I have yet to feel – nothing. But this? This was pain.

I am going to chalk it up to maybe I did too much. The only way to learn to walk is to walk. Maybe I went too far.

MY LLBFF IS COMING!!!!!

She is part of my heart. I want to say going through this BOOM journey has enhanced our relationship. No one but us will understand. If I could I would have crawled to get home, but when the time came to finally leave it was difficult to say good bye to those who God put in my life on this journey.

Bobbykins who made me PB&J and did my laundry, Pops who saw me coming off the trauma-hawk and was my escort anywhere I needed to be, my dear friend who brought normal to me, childhood and High School friends whose thoughts and prayers (& juice) gave me Ironman strength when I thought I had no more to give.

And my LLBFF who I cried with. I tried to be strong, to show everyone I could get through this. But there were times...and there were tears, and she was there.

Saying goodbye was difficult. Especially since I was leaving in a wheelchair with some crutches. I always thought when we saw each other next, I would be walking. Ok, not so much. Plan B. At least I will be able to stand on my own two feet long enough to give her a proper hug.

And we will make time go lightly, BOOM be damned. We will have a better visit than our last one.

*** technically the initial visit was great, it was the end (and prolonged stay) that sucked ***

MY NEW NEMESIS- THE STATIONARY BIKE

Conveniently we have a stationary bike in the guest room. Like most American homes 99% of the time it is used as a clothes rack. But with 2 active boys and a husband who does too much there is always a time someone was rehabbing.

My turn.

Per the doctor's instructions I raise the seat. Like Don Quixote facing the windmill I square off with the bike. Five minutes. I am allowed only five minutes of exercise. I need to do this. The muscle pain, the fact that this leg/hip still does not work is eating away at me. I need to do something.

Getting on is a feat in itself. The seat is so high, and I am being so careful.

Five minutes. It takes five minutes to get on and safely situate myself. I am dripping in sweat. I start to think – it took five minutes, does that mean I am done for the day? Nay nay I say again. Let's do this!

I start to pedal ever so slowly. But I learned from my pool excursion, don't over do this. So I stop/start/stop/start.

Ten minutes. It takes ten minutes to pedal for 5.

I need a shower, but a nap wins. I throw a towel on the bed and sleep on top of it to not drench my sheets in my sweat.

But I did it. I am working towards walking. I am doing something.

THE PAIN IS WORSE

I am worried. I call the surgeon's office. They say he is booked solid. I keep trying, telling them something is wrong. He said come back sooner if something is wrong. They need to get me in.

Two weeks. The best they can do is almost two weeks away.

I take it.

I scour through my meds to see how many painkillers and muscle relaxers I have – what do I have squirreled away? I can go two weeks if I cut them down and only take them at night.

John knows I am having pain. For better for worse, in sickness and health, he is here.

NOW I AM THE UBER DRIVER

A friend took me back and forth to work for months and we joked she was my Uber. LLBFF is coming and I will pick her up from the airport (only 15 minutes from my house). I told her I can't help with the bags, but I can drive that far.

I just can't get out of the car.

And her bags will need to go in the back seat as my walker is in the way back.

Will I ever be able to do anything normal again?

LLBFF IN THE HOUSE!

Literally. I needed a win. I needed my friend. I am exhausted but will make the most of our few days together. It may also give John a much-needed break.

CURSED

LLBFF's dad is seriously ill. She needs to get up North. She does not believe she will make it in time. I think back to when my sister was at her final days, and how hard it was to try and get there in time to say goodbye.

I tell her she has to try. She is breaking as she is on the phone.

I selfishly think we are fucking cursed. We are 2 for 2 in visits not ending well.

Meg-leg does not care my LLBFF is going through some serious shit. Fuck meg-leg, fuck the BOOM, fuck whoever put this curse on us.

I reset.

I silently pray – please let her get there and he be ok. *Please can we have a win?*

HE'S OK

Condensed version…

Planes trains automobiles LLBFF makes it. Specialist saves the day. Personally, I believe it was the intervention of her sister the nurse. She will spend time with her dad.

***side note: hospitals and health care sucks. ***

I am struggling. Will see the doctor soon.

INSURANCE SUCKS

Call one – test is being reviewed for coverage.

Call two – not covered.

Call three – covered.

Call four – not covered.

Multiple letters to the house.

A request for the surgeon to intervene for arbitration.

Insurance company feels all I need is 5 weeks of PT.

I tell them are they crazy? The idea of the test is to rule out something wrong we cannot see that potentially can cause me to break &/or tear something that may prove catastrophic. Can they look at my history? I tell them look for Humpty Dumpty, they see Ironman.

I call John's company and they will cover the test but let me know this will be it.

They need to rewrite the Rx and I wait again.

Finally schedule the test over lunch.

And I wait.

I HAVE NO PATIENCE

I know the guy who did the CT scan knows what's up. They check it before you leave.

You can't break them – they give up nothing.

I fill out paperwork, so every doctor gets the results.

I wait.

I hate waiting. I am waiting on my life. I am exhausted. I just want an answer. I want my shot.

By now the radiologist should have the report. I hear nothing.

Maybe there is an issue with the rewrite of the Rx. I call the surgeon's office today make sure they got the results.

Yes. But only the doctor can tell me. I have to wait for my appointment.

Did I say I hate waiting?

BROKEN IS TOO SOFT A WORD, PART 1

He was wrong. This surgeon who let me hope, who let me believe, who convinced me I was ok, was wrong.

I get to his office and wait, longer than usual. I don't know if I am imagining it, but I am not getting the friendly hellos as usual. I wait. As always, my results are up on the pc. I look at the picture but can't decipher it. There is a link to a supplemental file. My stomach is turning, and I think do I have time to click it myself? I wait.

The doctor comes in. I am hoping he says everything is fine, he was right, and he will just give me an injection. I notice the blinds are wide open. How can I get am injection with the blinds so open? Funny how you start to notice the smallest things. I look at him ready to ask if I should close the blinds.

Instead, he gives me the worst news – the bone did not grow into the cup of the prosthesis, and it has come loose. If it has not grown by now, it never will.

I try not to vomit.

I don't understand. How? Why?

Deja Vu. "It's nothing you did,"

I needed 30% bone to have the surgery. I had it. I had to have the surgery – the femoral head had collapsed. The Acetabulum was not great where the cup would eventually go. I was broken.

The femoral implant is fine. The ass-tablet has too much metal. The bone did not grow behind the cup.

I need surgery.

He needs to add a trauma surgeon. They need to remove ALL of the hardware. This is something beyond what he can do alone.

I break.

I breakdown.

I am shattered.

I cry like I had back at the BOOM. I cry like I did those first days in rehab. I cry worse than when I was told I needed a second surgery.

I am angry – I take it out (unfairly) on the doctor.

I tell him I knew; I knew something was wrong! But he was so sure…99.9% sure. I believed him – I had hope.

I tell him I called the office when they did not call with the results. He tells me his heart broke when he got the results and he could not tell me over the phone.

I tell him (loudly) Your heart broke? Am I supposed to feel bad for you?

I panic. **I CANNOT, WILL NOT GO BACK TO REHAB**.

I will do a Thelma and Louise off a cliff before I go back. I understand why they did it. The thought of what they faced offered no other way.

Then I panic more. There are no cliffs in Florida. I will have to drive far to get to a cliff. I can't drive more than half an hour. Why? Because I have a fucking broken hip.

I cry harder.

I tell him I count. I count everything. I am at 303 days. How do I go back to 1?

He is not done. I need bloodwork to see if the bone has an infection.

It is up to me when to have the surgery.

I will not get better, only progressively worse.

The pain will increase.

I must use the walker all of the time.

Eventually I will not be able to drive.

I was in a serious accident. I had major damage. I am broken.

There is more to tell, but not today.

Today – I … I can't.

BROKEN – PART 2

I couldn't make it out of the parking lot. I was having a panic attack. I went to the doctor by myself as I was only getting a shot. John is only down the street at work. I can make it down the street. If I call him this upset, he will drive uncontrollably to get to me. I cannot worry about him getting in an accident. I move my car to the end of the lot as I cry.

I am frozen. I can't go anywhere. I am alone and devastated. I just need to get calm enough to get down the street. I had sent John a series of texts from the doctor's office but got no response. I call my friends; I know they truly feel for me – I need comfort.

I get myself together enough to head on the road. I decide to stop at the bank first as I am still not 100%. I see my sisters from another mister (we just happened to be at the same place at the same time) and I lose it. I hug and cry and vent. I can't see John now. He can't see me broken again. I get it together and head home.

I call ahead to say I am on my way. John's folks are visiting and both kids are home. I tell them I'm stopping for lunch (to buy some time). While I wait at the restaurant, I start to search the internet for positive sides to being handicapped. I am handicapped. I saw a t-shirt with the handicap logo that states I Am Only In It For The Parking.

I order it. I laugh. I will be ok.

NOW WHAT?

Telling my family was hard. I let work know I would not be in. I need to process.

It's an understatement to say everyone is shocked.

In the midst of this I am being asked to come to come to New York to give a deposition for the BOOM. Do they not realize I can't even make it upstairs?

I have not mentioned the legal components to the BOOM. No one wants to cover your bills. You get a lawyer to do the paperwork so the insurance you have is forced to cover you – they feel it is the responsibility of the at fault party, who has not enough insurance to even cover my New York bills. In the case of any settlement the lawyer gets paid first, any outstanding medical bills get handled, the insurance company gets reimbursed, the line keeps going. I am expecting no payout and remain at a significant monetary loss in addition to what my life has become. At this point I have been paying all out-of-pocket expenses since I got back to Florida. I am out of pocket for medical, lost wages – pain and suffering accounts for nothing. You cannot get blood from a stone.

And the f'ing lawyer won't take a video deposition. He wants me in New York. I want to call him personally and video him what my life looks like. The need for adaptive tools, the inability to use a regular bathroom, the fact that I am living in my guest room. I want to scream at him what the pain feels like. He is being cruel. I was *sitting in the fucking backseat.*

I hate the driver. I hate the lawyer. I am filled with hate.

The doctor states I cannot travel. I laugh to myself. Not traveling is the least of what I cannot do.

PAIN

I have pain. Like all the time. Not BOOM pain, but now more than just discomfort. I am hobbling through life with broken bones. Eventually the screws will loosen and break if I do nothing.

I want to drink until I pass out. I don't. I don't even have one. I understand how you can spiral when something like this happens. I am 100% sure if I start down that path I will not return.

I hold a bottle with painkillers. I will take one. I could as easily swallow 10.

This painkiller does nothing. Two hours go by, and I feel a little groggy.

How do I live like this?

Should I go to the pain clinic – is that what my life has become? I research medical marijuana.

I can't. I can't live my life drugged up in bed. I need a plan.

PLAN F

You make a plan. It's doesn't work out. What's the plan B? If that doesn't work- plan C?

I'm up to plan F. For this fucking plan better work.

I'M NOT AN ACCOUNTANT – I REALLY DON'T EVEN PLAY ONE AT WORK

But I work in accounting with a fairly large staff. Know when we are busy? The end of the year and January. Remember when the BOOM happened and how long I was out of commission? Yeah, timing not so great. I am also trying to layer in life. Things that John and I need to do.

I missed my son's first semester at college. We dropped him off and a few weeks later… well let's not rehash that. I really have not been able to go anywhere. And now? I barely want to leave bed sometimes.

So it looks like the stars can align for the end of October. I will miss another Halloween. I have given up celebrating.

This time feels different. Obviously, you can't plan for a BOOM. The second surgery happened so fast after returning home I was still riding the crazy train. Now? Now I have time to plan.

And I'm scared. If you have time to think your mind can be vicious. I have a gut feeling this is not going to have a happy outcome.

I tell no one.

I plan. Plan S – S for Secret. S for Shit Happens. It is my plan and my plan alone.

EVERYONE IS CRAZY

I can't tell you how many people want/need things from me. If I had 6 months, I could not get it all done. There is no rest for the wicked. They are all f'ing crazy.

Our son will be moving into his first apartment off campus. I will drag my broken ass tablet across the state to see it. I won't be able to help with anything, but I want to see it. It may be my only time. I want to make up for everything I missed. This crazy is mine.

Accidents all over I-95 this week. People don't know how to Drive (obviously). Crazy Drivers.

THE KID'S PLACE

I want to live here. It's beautiful. He and his roommates are the first residents in this phase of new construction. He has his own bathroom bigger than the one I am using and a walk-in closet.

The ride was rough, but I tried not to let it show. It's not long, but long for me. "We" do shopping for his new digs, which means I find a place in the store to sit while they get everything. Even that becomes too much for me. We are staying a few days (I finally am using PTO for something other doctors and hospitals). At one point I tell John take me back to the hotel – I just can't. This is the first time since the BOOM he seems annoyed. I have a feeling he would have rather I opted out of this trip. I don't tell him why I insisted I needed to come. He takes me back.

We have some meals together, spend some time in his place as they set everything up and unpack. I am satisfied. Should anything happen he has what he needs. He can just renew the lease and stay here until graduation.

PS – Other son is fine. Has a decent job and living at home for now.

All is good. Plan S.

WHAT WOULD I DO WITHOUT MEDICAL INSURANCE?

As I stated before the asswipe who did this to me (he who WILL NEVER BE NAMED) doesn't have much.

Legal lesson expanded Let's say you are lucky enough to have health coverage like I do. But you have a BOOM. Is that the fault of your insurance carrier? No, of course not. That's what they say too. Then they say, "why should I pay when it's not my fault?" (IC= Insurance Carrier)

Me: Because that's why I have insurance. To cover my doctor, hospital, etc. when I need it.

IC: Nay nay is the response.

IC: Get it from the other guy.

Me: How?

IC: Sue him.

Me: That may take years and I don't know if he even has five cents.

IC: We will be kind enough to pay *BUT* we will have a subrogation lien against any future settlements (i.e. – anything you get is ours until we are fully repaid).

They are not the only lien I have. Nor are all my bills paid. And I have a shit ton of out-of-pocket expenses. You have to deal with EVERY person in the accounting offices as soon as they know you had a crash. It adds hours to something as simple as making appointments. You sign away your life, pay all your deductibles UP FRONT and promise to pay if the insurance company decides not to, after they said they will.

Legal lesson over.

Back to my day. It feels like I am making 50 appointments. I have to have "follow ups" with all the doctors first to assess me and my progress. Then I need to schedule pre-ops closer to the date. Which I don't have because I can't schedule until everyone else sees me and say "you look ok enough."

Just another year I will meet my high deductible as well as my out-of-pocket max.

BREATHE DEEP…

Or put a pillow over my head. I'm not sure which one to do.

I mentioned a plan. The need to plan. AGAIN. Ironman is back today so I need to take advantage of that. I call the surgeons office – AGAIN. I call him more than anyone else I know. Someday I hope to delete his number. Today is not that day.

I state we talked about a Trauma Surgeon, but realistically after my tirade and threat to drive off a cliff, the rest of the visit was akin to when the teacher is talking in a Charlie Brown cartoon- waa waa waa waa.

I get the information for the guy who will be doing the reverse Frankenstein part of my surgery- he needs to deconstruct the erector set in my hip and ass tablet. The fact my guy says this is far beyond his capabilities makes me nervous. If this is done wrong, it may take away my chances of ever walking again. The bones just do NOT cooperate.

I will also have to see my primary, the cardio, the rheumatologist, the mailman, and the person at the drive thru at Dunkin' Donuts to name a few. Ok, maybe not the mailman. But you get the idea. This is an ordeal that requires coordination. Have I mentioned before my *lack of coordination?*

At least when you are unconscious and in a Trauma center you have people that handle this kind of shit for you. Now? I am that people.

For anyone who works, trying to coordinate a meeting with more than 4 people is a nightmare. Try to coordinate this mess. Mercury has to line up with 5 stars and 4 planets while a Comet Storm passes through for everyone to make this happen.

Oh by the way, remember I am working full time again. And I am in pain. Great. Just f'ing great.

Sitting with a calendar, a pad, and a bunch of phone numbers as I start Plan F.

MY FRIEND THE INTERNET

When I was a kid my mother's most prized possession was a set of Encyclopedias. Any question that came up and we would go to the bookcase and lookup the answer. I was surprised she let us touch them without gloves.

Now I am researching my deconstruction. I scour the dates of the papers for the most up to date research. I look for success percentages. I gather my questions. This time there will be no surprises. I plan. I am informed.

So far, the doctors' appointments are going well. However let me offer you some advice. Make a video of your answers so you don't have to repeat yourself 1,000 times. To nurses, PAs, doctors, people in the waiting room. It zaps your strength.

Dr. Trauma, the removal specialist is confident on taking me apart. He tells me how long his part will be – less time than I spent in his waiting room.

When you are hospitalized or in rehab, you have nothing but time. And you are in or near a bed 90% of the time. This? Going to see the doctors? Waiting rooms? Exhausting. Waste of my time. Did I say exhausting? Can't remember – you know I was in a serious accident and had two surgeries…

Not going to keep boring you with my groundhog existence if there is nothing new. Just close your eyes and imagine being tired, going to work, going to doctors, sitting in waiting rooms, explaining the same thing over and over, having tests ordered, being poked and prodded, and dreaming of bed. This will be my life until the surgery. Oh yeah, don't forget that every day the prosthesis pulls farther and farther away from my bone and the screws loosen on their way to breaking (i.e. there is pain).

DAY 365 CRASHAVERSARY IS A THING

Today is my full Crashaversary, the first anniversary of the BOOM that changed not only my life, but so many close to me. I will admit I had a rough night thinking about today coming. I thought about my losses. I thought how I had hoped after several surgeries I would be walking unaided by now, of my need for yet another operation. I thought of John – how I could not have made it through this last year without everything he does for me. He definitely got the worse out of the for better or worse part of our vows. I say that often, and at the same time maybe not often enough.

And I thought of everyone else who helped me along this last year's journey starting with strangers holding my hand in the ER & hugs from the EMT, to the many prayers, visits in the rehab center, funny gifts to lift my spirit, actual food to replace the prison slop I was served. The gift of time from so many who tried to bring normal to my nightmare. The late-night texts, the calls, the cards. The juice and coffee. The hugs when words did not suffice. The sacrifices made by my family – from needing my laundry done to missing Holidays.

I am forever changed. I am forever grateful. (I am Ironman).

While these are only words and it does not seem enough, thank you to everyone for helping me though the darkness.

I'M NOT AN ACCOUNTANT – PART 2

After the BOOM John and discussed seeing a financial planner. I've spoken to some before, but they don't like the way we live our life.

That's a funny statement if you know us. We live in the same house for like 18 years. We do have newer cars, but that is because John works for a distributor and we get killer lease deals.

We choose to pay for our son's educations (undergraduate or trade-their choice). We want them both to have a good education and not worry about loans. That is our choice as parents. We feel if you decide to have a family, you should be prepared to support them within your means. Again, this was our choice. So instead of vacations, we put money into college funds. Instead of moving to a nicer house, better neighborhood, we stay in our home.

Some financial planners think that is wrong. Several told me how we need to worry about US, OUR RETIREMENT. I told them I need to worry about my boys. Obviously, I did not sign with any of them.

As John is crazy busy, I have volunteered to handle this part of our lives. I don't tell him because my gut is saying get your affairs in order.

So again, I gather all information and start to have meetings with a planner that is recommended and whom I am told will listen.

I like her. She is young, bright, and personable. She sees the golden chariot and spends time getting to know me. We barely talked business the first few meetings. I trust her.

Then I tell her I need plans. Note the S at the end. I need a plan if I don't make it out of surgery. I need a plan if I can't walk. And I need the plan I hope to use, I have some aspect of normalcy. I sign papers. I have John just sign what I put in front of him. If we don't finalize everything before the surgery, I will leave instructions with John on how he should enact my plan.

I make sure there is cash in an account to cover the costs of college, apartment, books, fees, etc. through graduation. I make sure there is ready cash for whatever. I make sure there is money for a nice service just in case. Plan S.

NERVOUS

Getting closer to surgery. I am nervous. I can't be nervous. Where did Ironman go?

HOW DO YOU TURN OFF THE WORLD?

As my time grows near (see every thought is morose) people are reaching out. Trying to connect. Everyone is still a part of this journey.

They don't realize I am like a prizefighter the week of the big fight. I need to focus. I can't be distracted. I need to make sure my t's are crossed and i's dotted. I have to make sure I have done right by everyone who supported me. John, the kids, my friends, my job.

I have to breathe. I have to pray. I have to hope.

I can't talk to everyone. Actually, I can't talk to anyone. I text. In some cases I just copy and paste my reply. If I take these calls I will break – shatter. I am already broken; it won't take much to finish the job.

I can't expel the energy needed to fake my way through. This time I am not drawing on their strength – this time the contact has an opposite effect.

I just want to walk.

PARDON ME – BUT TODAY IS UN-FUCKING BELIEVABLE

Tomorrow is surgery.

Nope. It's not.

Apparently, no one has the results of a test I know I took. That doctor's office is not answering their phone. The hospital in their infinite last minute check list said we cannot proceed without this test. We will have to reschedule.

No fucking way.

I am as ready as I will ever be. I won't be this ready again.

I am at work – I now stop everything as I am making calls.

We give up and my primary says come in now – I will do the test here. My anxiety has hit max level 100. I race (for me) there.

I fail the test. They cannot get me to calm down. I am having a nervous breakdown. More calls.

The hospital agrees that my anxiety is an issue. They would be willing to retest right before surgery if I come for a blood work up. NOW.

Off to the hospital. Waiting room, blood test, then, surprise... don't leave the area. My blood pressure has skyrocketed and they are worrying I am having a heart attack. All indications are probably not, but you never know. They add another blood test. They say if that comes back positive, they need to admit me.

I tell them they are giving me a fucking heart attack. I am close to the office, so I go back there to wait and pack up my stuff.

I call John. I have been updating him throughout the day. His stress level equals mine. We can't reschedule.

While waiting for results the cardio calls. Asks did I stop certain meds. Said yes, the hospital said stop them last night. Winner winner chicken dinner. That combined with anxiety is most likely the reason for bad results. But we have to wait for results anyway.

Tick. Tick. Tick. Tick.

I get the call. I am good to go. I go home.

My bag is packed, I take my first pre-op shower with the most God awful disinfectant. I answer only 2 texts.

I can't sleep.

I WILL NOT THROW UP I WILL NOT THROW UP

Second disgusting shower and off we will be going.

DO I SAY THIS IS DAY 1 OR DAY 406?

Surgery went well apparently. I am in a private room at the end of the hall – don't know how I scored that.

We got to the hospital, they redid the test (passed) and a host of doctors came in and out to see me prior to surgery. They were all waiting for the test results to see if we were a go. I was "supposed" to make sure someone called the cardio – but hey, that's not my job.

The surgeon tells me (again- Deja vu) that he feels the length is pretty spot on. Not only did I have to have hardware removed, but the space in the ass tablet where the cup was needed to be dug deeper. The femoral head of the prosthesis gets replaced too. The Dr. actually showed me on a model how it's done. Pretty cool. Everything is coming up roses!

Tells me removal was great – three screws were broken. Now I know why the pain was so bad.

Speaking of which – aside from surgical pain – I am feeling pretty good. Unlike the last time where he went in through the front, this surgery required them to recut through the original scar. Maybe a zipper would have been prudent. This time no staples. Hmmm.

I will be out of bed today. Start PT and be home in a few days. Nurse and PT at the house, same drill as before.

My gut was wrong. Everything is fine. I am fine.

SURPRISE DOCTOR VISIT AT NIGHT

My primary pops in after 10 pm. He wants to see how I am doing. Checks the charts. Asks me what happened to my heart.

"What happened to my heart?", WHAT HAPPENED TO MY HEART?!

There is a note that it looks like it stopped at some point. He is going to see what that is about. That would probably explain these giant pads on my chest.

You would think that is something they would tell me.

No one knows anything.

When I see the cardio I ask him. He doesn't know. He is still asking why no one called him. I tell him I spoke to someone and thought he was calling him. Oops.

I CAN DO PT BY MYSELF IF THEY LET ME

Let me start by saying after the surgery, I was able to use the bathroom on my own straight out of the gate. Just needed a watcher.

PT was even easier. They were amazed how well I did. When I explain my 2 months in jail, sorry rehab and first surgery they get it. I even do the baby steps. At this rate I can be home tomorrow.

Also – pain is gone. Just surgical discomfort.

GROUNDHOG DAY – YET AGAIN.

I'm home. Nurse and PT will be coming. I feel better than I have in a long while. Nurse says everything looks good. Leaves some bandages for us to change if need be before I see her again.

PT makes me do the dog and pony show to make sure I don't hurt myself. She is out in record time. She will be back and says we will be walking.

I GET GOLD STARS IN PT

I am using the walker. She has me up and walking around the downstairs. AGAIN – the only way to relearn to walk is to walk. There is no strength training as we can't pull at the surgical site. My job is to walk several times a day.

The week progressed well. I am kicking ass and taking names. She even let me walk outside (with of course her holding onto my shorts). Because I again have surgical restrictions I can't bend, lift, etc. So my life is these little walks.

Nurse keeps coming, everything is healing excellent. I look with a mirror, scar is AMAZING. I text friends pictures. It's surreal.

The PT can't believe how well I am doing. She is confident I will be walking unaided eventually. She says I really don't need her. She wants to do the stairs with me before she stops her sessions.

I pause. Stairs? Um no.

She says I am here, let's try. We go, albeit slowly. Good goes to heaven. I get to the top and ask her can I go see my bathroom? She thinks I have to go. I tell her no, and explain we had a leak, and the vanity needed to be replaced and I've only seen pictures. I explain I live downstairs but being since we are here….

She asks if she can come too. We both love the bathroom. She will come one more time after my 2 week check up and I will be discharged from PT.

MY LIFE WENT NUCLEAR

Everything was going well. Too well. I took a long walk with no pain. I cried, but after this long ordeal they were tears of joy. I called my friend to tell her I was happy crying. This is almost over.

Johnny drove me to my checkup. Smiles and pats on the back all around.

The surgeon slightly moves my leg. Ouch.

Ouch?

I said "Well that was uncomfortable". Attribute this to getting in car and coming out. Everything looks good and we are off.

My groin is uncomfortable on the way home. By the time we get there I need a painkiller. Ok, so my first outing took too much out of me.

I wake up and need another pain killer. Back to sleep.

I wake up and can't move. I am calling the doctor as John comes to check on me and tells me to call. I show him the phone in my hand.

"Can you get to the hospital?"

Uh oh.

He says everything was fine today. This is most likely muscular, and the hospital will check. They will then be able to give me something for the pain until it subsides. Off we go.

No, we don't. 10 minutes later and I am screaming as I can't get in the car the pain is so bad. I finally get in before we call an ambulance.

When I get to the hospital I can't get out of the car. I am in a wheelchair and taken though emergency. I need help to get on the bed. They think maybe the hip dislocated. I told them I am careful and follow protocol. Not knowing me they look doubtful.

I need X-rays. I can't get out of this bed. They wheel me bed and all to X-ray. We wait.

A nurse comes by to tell me about my admission. What? She tells me I need surgery.

What the fuck?

She realizes the doctor didn't tell me and goes and gets him. He comes back with my X-rays and says he can tell something is wrong, but doesn't know what. He said he called the surgeon who looked at the X-rays. It was him who told them to admit me and schedule surgery. I will be operated on exactly 2 weeks to the day from the last surgery.

I DON'T KNOW HOW TO EVEN COUNT ANYMORE

Is this Day 1? Or Day 14? Or day 420?

I sent John home and told him I will call when I know when my surgery is scheduled. He needs some sleep.

I text and call a friend. And yes, I cry. I can't. I just can't. AGAIN

I use that word a lot here. AGAIN. I am starting to hate that word.

The doctor comes in somewhere around 6. I look him straight in the eye and say, *"WHAT THE FUCK HAPPENED?"*

The cup came out. He has no idea how or why. He won't know until he opens me up (*note. I said I needed a zipper, now that is not so funny). He says he has no choice but to go back in.

I ask him why he thinks he can fix me now. He looks forlorn. He said he will fix me. Gives me my surgical time and says will see me later.

Not too much later my friend shows up uninvited and unannounced but desperately needed. She sits by the side of my bed to hold my hand as I cry. She doesn't want me to be alone. She will stay with me until John comes. Same situation, 420 days apart. Someone holding my hand in a hospital.

I don't know why, but I show her my scar and comment how well it healed. And now they are going to cut me open again.

John comes, and off I go.

I WOULDN'T BELIEVE YOU IF YOU SAID THE SKY WAS BLUE

I wake up in my room again (not as nice as last time). John is there and I am groggy. I ask him questions, he answers. I think I ask him again. He is annoyed. I send him home. I think we have reached our breaking point.

The next morning the surgeon comes in.

The bone died. It was alive, but it died. Then the cup fell out.

What is different now? He drilled into the bone to make sure he had good blood flow, then he poked around a bit. The bone came apart. He kept on keeping on. I started with a 32mm cup. I ended up with a 54mm cup in a 52mm opening (to jam it in). That's how much bad bone there was. I had 3 units of blood.

You all do realize I was in a serious accident?

He then used bone graft putty (which sounds cheap but when I look at the EOBs is surprisingly expensive). He put in a bunch of screws for good measure. He then added an Oh My God screw, because, well I have no luck. Then he said I was back to no weight bearing. Drop the mic.

That means wheelchair.

Two months. It is day 1. AGAIN

NO NO NO

I was not kidding when I said I was not going back to rehab. I am in despair.

They will send a PT to the house to assess if I can handle it. I plan on acing that test. Or I will knock the PT out. Visiting nurse yet again.

How am I going to manage this? I have to figure out how I can have a support system without having John run himself in the ground. I also need him not to be around me 24 hours a day.

Doesn't take long for the news to spread. I can't tell you how many people volunteered to babysit me.

Either I rely on this generous group, or I potentially am back in a rehab center. Good news is my no weight bearing time coincides with the holiday season. There are planned vacations, time when the boys will be here. This may be doable. If I can get past needing help.

I'm not going back. I ask for help. EVERYONE helps. I mean EVERYONE. A schedule is made.

I pass the assessment. There is some dispute over my method for showering. I nod in agreement but will do it my way as I know I can do it. The PT comes back to check on me, but given the circumstances there is nothing I can do. PT is done.

The incision bleeds through. I don't think my hip was meant to be opened so many times. Unfortunately, on one of Johnny's babysitting days he has to change the bandage which is now stuck. The look on his face haunts me. I won't make him do it again.

THANKSGIVING

Everyone is home for Thanksgiving. We are finally all under the same roof again. You can barely see the chair in a picture I take with the boys. It will have to do.

I am thankful. Additional words cannot enhance that sentiment.

EVERY BABYSITTER IS DIFFERENT

Yet I love them all.

Obviously, John is wonderful- but I worry about him. This is too much, and he can't relax around me. Sometimes I just go to bed so he can take a break.

Older son is great. He tends to distance, but make sure I have my phone to text him, and then he checks on me like clockwork. He does not hover but is close every time I need something. He also takes me to my doctors' appointments.

I have babysitters who if you could ignore the wheelchair, you wouldn't know were babysitting. They save me as it is the only time I get to feel normal. I can't put a price on that.

I have huggers. They show up when I tend to need them the most.

THE HALLMARK CHANNEL AND OTHER MINDLESS SHOWS

It's hard to concentrate. I also nap often. I am up at odd times. None of this makes for good tv/movie watching. It's annoying to put something on only to fall asleep and have to rewind, then repeat.

Welcome to The Hallmark Channel, which is much better than the Gameshow Network rehab roommate was obsessed with. I can and do watch this 24/7. Until one of the babysitters introduces me to the 90 Day Fiancé franchise.

Now I get it why people stare. You can't help but be mesmerized by someone's train wreck of a life.

GOIN' HUNTING

Not me.

Last year was to be our younger son's first hunting trip. Due to the BOOM it was canceled. I don't want to be the cause of him not going again.

I broach the subject with John, and he shuts me down. He doesn't want to be far away from me. But he needs this trip too.

I reach out to the babysitter club and ask for volunteers so they can go hunting for a few days. I am getting better at asking for help. We make a schedule- including overnight coverage when my other son is working.

John says no.

I persevere. They will be going.

PSA ON BABYSITTERS LETTING KIDS WATCH TOO MUCH TV

I can only speak as the mother of boys. They watched a lot of TV and movies. But most of the time it was just background noise. They liked action figures and Legos.

Notable exception. When our oldest was little he loved The Lion King. Over and over and over. We finally put a tv and VCR in his room and showed him how to rewind it. If I heard "hey ya" one more time I would have lost it.

I mentioned the Hallmark Channel. I have watched so many Christmas shows I developed an algorithm to write them. You choose one from each category. Blonde or Brunette? Big city gal stuck in a small midwestern town or stoic businessman who only lives to work? Do the main characters meet on a plane or is the flight canceled and they band together to get to their destinations?

Will she lose the Christmas Tree Farm – Toy Store – Apple Orchard? Were they high school sweethearts who haven't seen each other in years or is he on leave from the service? Definitely found my next job.

My babysitters humor me. I have become a dumb smart person.

EVERYTHING AT ARM'S REACH

John is trying to make things easy for me. We still live on different floors. We have people in and out of our home taking shifts with me.

He is worried I will need something, and he will not be here. He puts everything I could ever need in reach of my wheelchair. Each morning he places a fresh coffee cup on the counter. He makes sure the coffee maker is moved closer within reach. He puts plates/bowls out. Cereal stays on the table. Everywhere you look there is something I could use 3 feet off the ground.

I have all the restrictions as after the BOOM. He makes sure there is enough milk in a separate container for me easily in reach in the refrigerator.

Do you know a gallon of milk weighs over 8 pounds? I will have no more than a 5-pound restriction. Right now, I don't even have that.

Adaptive tools have been ever present. But now there are more grabbers in various rooms. Furniture is moved so I can get around in this oversized chair.

The worst part – I am required to use the f'ing stabilizer pillow anytime I am not sitting. I did make a deal with the surgeon in the hospital. I will use it but refuse to be strapped in. I place the torture device and use a heavy blanket over it.

I have lost the ability to sleep in any other position than on my back. AGAIN. Someday….

The chair is too wide to get into the bedroom or bathroom. Just like rehab, I transfer from the chair to a one-legged stand and use the walker. I will need to work my way back to crutches.

I do what I have to. This may be my last hope. Ironman don't leave me now.

OUTSIDE

I can't go outside. I spend my days in bed or in that chair. My limited mobility does not allow me to get on my patio even with assistance. I open the slider, and wheel up to the door. If I'm lucky I can feel a breeze. I can see a bit more of the world. I can hear the birds. The dogs love that they are not stuck in the house. I joke as I stuck my leg through the doorway from my chair – I'm in, I'm out.

If this is permanent, we need to have ramps added. I can't be stuck in here.

If this is permanent, we may have to move.

If…

Right now, I miss outside. I am miserable but am trying to hide it.

I DON'T WRITE ABOUT EVERYTHING

I didn't write about my anniversary. I didn't write about Christmas. Some days are good and normal – and for me.

I didn't write about how I had to cut socks because the swelling was too much, I couldn't get them on. I didn't write about how I hate sleeping only on my back. I didn't write about so many things. There are days that I am struggling. But the truth is how I feel most days is so repetitious. What more is there to say?

Am I losing my voice? Did I get this far only to get stuck? I'm tired. How many times can I say it?

469 – 4 – 1

A.M. Start of the day 469

By now you know I count. Numbers equate to days. Numbers have meaning – to me, to my life, to the BOOM.

I have not walked unaided now for 469 days. Let that settle in. Today I will meet with the surgeon to see if this bone has chosen life or death. I can only pray this small section of my body chooses life. I hang by a thread in the balance.

My babysitters – AKA my family, my caregivers, my cheerleaders, my heart – they are nothing but positive as they watch me. They say all the right words, but I know too how they feel deep inside – what if? They never show anything but positivity, as if any wrong action or word on their part will doom the outcome. No one will do anything to jinx the outcome. Will it be enough? I don't know.

I have been sooooo careful. I leave nothing to chance. Except for the doctor and hospital I have been in the house for over 2 months. While it is better than rehab I am still in prison. If the bone dies – I just don't know. My son will take me today to learn my fate. John will wait at home. It's better this way. Neither of us will survive if the news is bad. We will need to process separately before we plan together.

I put on a brave face and off we go.

Afternoon 4

We are at the doctors. I always come at the same time as directed by the staff in the back. I am always first. The girls at the desk always comment that my appointment is for later – they don't get I am a special case. The nurses are vested in the outcome. As always, I am first when he gets in from the hospital.

Room – x-rays- wait. This has been repeated more times than I can count. I explain to then assistant my areas of weakness and discomfort. We make sure they are x-rayed.

We wait for the doctor. He comes in smiling and shakes my hand.

The moment of truth.

**** INSERT DRAMATIC PAUSE HERE ******

THE BONE DID NOT DIE!

I don't believe him. We go through the X-ray. We go through months of x-rays. We blow up the pictures. I ask question after question. He was sure before – how can he be sure now?

The bone is alive. The screws are in place. The prosthetic has not moved.

My heart starts to beat again.

We discuss the need for a shot to help with swelling, pain and weakness. When that kicks in in a few days I can try the cane again. The walker will go. He thinks the cane will go. He says the next time I see him I will just be walking. He has to make me believe so I will continue the fight the next few months to finish strong.

I didn't come this far to give up. Three months. I have a plan for the next three months. The bone will grow for 12 – 18 months total. I will nurture it during the duration. I can deal with the spasms and the swelling for the next two to three months. I can deal with the discomfort. I will finish strong.

In the office I let go of the walker and take 4 steps toward the doctor. Wobbly, old age steps. But without an aid of any kind or holding onto to a counter or table or person. FOUR honest to God real steps. He shakes my hand and smiles. I will see him in three months. Not two weeks – THREE months. We expect that to be my last visit. I will need a yearly checkup indefinitely, but that will be like a visit to an old friend. I can go home. I can go to work. I can go out. I can go home.

I call John. I hear the relief in his voice. I am coming home.

I text my babysitters – they are all fired. They all express their joy with me – I am Ironman yet again. For someone who has been very verbose in chronicling this journey I at a loss for words to express how I feel about them. Right now, my soul is soaring.

I came home and we call John's folks. It is great to share good news. I call and text everyone who have been waiting to hear. I end the year on a positive note.

Next 1

I am not naive to say this journey is over. I still have a big hill to climb in front of me. My leg and hip have to learn to walk again. It will take several months. I will need to remain ever diligent to not do anything stupid to jeopardize the healing. I have to follow the doctor's orders. I have to take the muscle relaxers a bit more than I have been. I will continue with the massage cream and try and work these muscles and scar tissue. I also have constant pins and needles. Constant. Sometimes it is worse and coupled with cramps, but it never goes away. There is nothing to be done for that.

Some things will not change for a long time, some maybe ever. I am a long way away from using the stairs. I still will not be able to just walk into a shower. I cannot bend and tie my laces. I will need the comfort and support of sneakers as I begin my foray back into using two legs. I will most likely have the need of these adaptive tools for at least the next year, possibly forever. The scars are healing, but they will be a constant reminder of the BOOM and all that came from it. I will carry hope that the healing continues.

I dream of someday – someday (hopefully) filled with grandchildren. While I won't be able to chase them around or go on rollercoasters, I will be able to take them to all sorts of wonderful places.

I dream of John, and I being retired someday – and taking a leisurely stroll down a small-town Main Street to dinner.

I dream of someday just taking my dog for a walk.

I dream of someday getting out of my car and walking into a store from the parking lot.

I dream of someday walking to get the mail.

I dream of someday being able to get a glass of water from the kitchen and carry it to the table.

I have dreams both big and small – and right now they are all someday.

Tomorrow is DAY 1. I am not going to count the continuation of the BOOM. I am going to count my recovery and my road to walking.

PS: I find it poetic that my day 1 is the start of the new year. When I think back at the last year I am glad it is in the rear view mirror. But there are things to remember. The love I felt. How grateful I am to be blessed with the people God put in my path. To finally learn to ask and accept help.

BACK TO WORK

I have been working from home part time AGAIN. I have now received a release so I can go back in the office.

Back to the golden chariot. Then the cane. I'm tired all the time. Walking is exhausting me.

My life mocks me. All I want is to walk. Walking sucks the life from me. And I dread it.

How do I reconcile this? At least I am out of the house.

COVID 19

People are getting sick and dying. Everywhere. This is exactly the plot of a Matt Damon movie.

Our company will be having all our team members work from home. We are trying to figure out how. We are not a company that works that way. It was not an easy decision. Our leadership team made a plan. Then changed it. Then changed it again. No one could have planned for this. BOOM.

Sound familiar?

LOCKDOWN

The world is in lockdown. Like everyone I am scared.

Yet unlike everyone I am selfishly pissed. In essence I have been in lockdown since the BOOM. Now that I am on a road to recovery a global pandemic makes me a prisoner again. I am embarrassed that I can even think this. Who am I?

THE POOL

It's been almost 4 1/2 months since my last surgery. Decided to test out the pool today. While it was still a bit on the cool side, I was able to get in with my cane. Not going to push my luck and try swimming, but the relief on my hip/side was amazing. You don't realize how much pressure gravity puts on it, sitting, standing or even laying down. It was the most relief I have had in months.

Once I was in, I used the cane to go a little deeper before I set it aside on the pool deck. The weightlessness of the water let me stand unaided - which was surreal. I tentatively took a step. 555 Days since I last took a step unaided. I took a few more. I can actually visualize myself walking one day.

Update: my excitement got the best of me. I think I understand how astronauts feel like when they return to earth. Gravity is a bitch. I **soooo** overdid it today and now that I have been out of the water, I feel it. I am in bed. I have to learn balance.

I CAN'T SWIM

Don't get me wrong, I know how. Or I did. I have been in the pool every chance I get. I am able to move the meg-leg in ways I couldn't or haven't since the BOOM. Not only does it feel good, but I am seeing the progress.

I started by taking tentative steps in the water. I slowly increased the number each time. Then I started making major milestones. 100, 200, 300, 600. It was not fast, and certainly not pretty. But it is effective.

I decided I was strong enough to try and swim. Not so much. Sunk to the bottom. Apparently, you need to know how to swim with only one good side.

Eventually.

NOTHING

Nothing has changed. I meander around the first floor of our house. I work at the kitchen table. John is trying different places to work. The world is crumbling.

I don't see any progress with my ass tablet. I am worried about the boys. One will be staying in his apartment at college as the number of COVID cases is much less where he is. I will not see him for who knows how long. AGAIN.

MY SECOND FATHER

Our family is devastated – crushed – broken – shattered. John's father passed away – a victim of COVID.

He cannot travel to be with his family. His mother and sister are under quarantine as we all anxiously await to see if this horror has waged war on them as well.

There can be no service. This faceless demon has taken our heart. I don't know how to comfort him. How much more of a burden can he bear? There were no goodbyes. It all happened so fast. BOOM.

He was alone. This man who gave everything to all, who was always there for everyone, died alone. How can that be? He deserved better, he deserved more. He deserved everything.

I left home under less-than-ideal circumstances. John's family took me in without a second thought. I lived with them until we were married. Pops stood with John and me as I packed the few things I would take. There were no words spoken, but the warmth of his love gave me strength.

I don't think I ever told him, but I almost asked him to give me away at our wedding. It was a difficult decision for me. I ultimately chose my uncle.

When my father died, my uncle had come to me and said if ever there was a time I needed a father, come to him. If there was every anything I would ask my father, ask him. He was the only one to talk to me about my father dying. He took the time to comfort a 14-year-old girl. I believed and never forgot his words.

But John's dad did not offer to step in for my father, he just became my dad too. I did not ask because I thought it would be unfair to him. If I asked, he would have said yes. He needed to be with his family – I wouldn't take that away from him or them. When we watched the video of our wedding, there was a section where guests recorded messages. I can still hear his words, "To my son and daughter..."

I could write thousands upon thousands of words about this man, and you still would not understand how special he was. I don't think words have been invented yet to do him justice. BOOM – Your world changes in an instant.

When my BOOM happened, he came to the trauma center and was there when I was taken from the helicopter. He told me about it on a visit at rehab once. As we talked about that day, I could see he paused – with a stop of his breath and a tear in his eye. I am so sorry I was the cause of any pain he had.

He generally came for visits with John's mom. But on a few occasions, he came alone. On those days he would sneak around outside of the rehab room to peek in and see how I was doing. He would smile – a smile from his heart – when he saw how hard I was working and the progress I was making. Against the rules, they would say "Your father is here" and let him in the room with me.

How is it fair that this man was ripped from our family and people like the driver of the other car is still here? Where is the justice? How much more can we take?

John needs time to process. We are in lockdown. There is nowhere for him to go. I offer to go tell our son. This is something we will not do over the phone. I tell him our oldest will drive me. It will take about 2 1/2 hours, the longest I will be in a car. He agrees – that is how badly he needs some alone time. It is the only thing I can do for him.

I take muscle relaxers and bring painkillers with me. My son will only hear about his Grandfather's death from us. He has spent too much time alone processing bad news.

**** Update: I won't say John's mom and sister are fine. No one is fine. I will say they do not have COVID ***

I CAN'T COOK

So, everyone who knows me is shaking their head in agreement at that statement. There are a number of things I can do, but cooking is not even on the bottom of the list – it is on a list all its own. I can make almost anything that comes from a box, I know how to boil water, and I can make tacos and pizza bagels.

Yet being handicapped prohibits you from even doing basic things. The unsteadiness, only having one available hand, the inability to stand for any length of time. The stupid restrictions. The necessary restrictions.

After one of the many surgeries, the doctor gave me a typed list of things NOT to do. Most made sense, some I wouldn't have thought of. Lifting a gallon of milk? Nope. It weighs over 8 pounds. Sleeping on your side? Could not even if I tried. Cooking? Again, no.

Wait – do I have it in writing I am NOT to cook? I may need to frame this. I finally have an excuse.

We are trapped. Physically and emotionally right now. I need to do **something.**

Today I was able to fry an egg – for me that's cooking. It has taken me this long to work up enough stamina and strength to stand at the stove with my cane, leaning in the counter when needed, just to fry an egg. I need a nap.

SWIMMING

It was starting to piss me off being in the pool so much and regulated to the shallows (aka baby end). I stare down the rest of the water, which mocks me.

My sister taught me how to swim. That's actually not a true statement. She threw me in the water at Jones Beach, and each time I struggled back to shore, choking, spitting out water, she threw me back. She felt that our mother babied me. That all of the time my mom was trying to teach me to swim, there was no real motivation. Drowning, or almost drowning, appeared to be that motivation. After I got the hang of it, we would swim farther and farther out, throwing a football that we could cling to as a makeshift float if we needed a break. Mom would have had a heart attack if she saw how we spent those days at the beach.

As a kid in The Bronx, we belonged to a pool club. The place was huge and had several large community pools plus tons of daily activities; paddle ball, crafts, basketball, shuffleboard – the list goes on. We would spend most days of the summer there. The same families sitting in "their spots" year after year. My mom would never come looking for us – it was a safe place. Kids ran themselves ragged outdoors in the sun until we were on the verge of collapse at the days end, only to repeat it the next day.

I was enthralled by the diving boards. My mother made me practice diving from the edge of the deep end countless days before she felt it was safe for me to try even the low board. It was always the highlight of my days. I wasn't very coordinated - a fact that carries throughout my life, but I loved the feeling of cutting into the water.

So now in my own backyard in a much smaller pool, I have come to the realization that with my injuries I will most likely never be able to dive in the water again. Before the BOOM I couldn't tell you if I ever used the steps getting in unless I was with the kids when they were little. It's yet another thing taken away from me. That list just keeps on growing.

I am determined that I will swim. Today is the day. I can hear my mother's voice back when she was trying, "swim little fishy". I smile, but it is the memory of my sister throwing me in the ocean that lets me know I am strong enough to do this. Off I go.

While my right leg is not actually helping, it is no longer hindering me. My arms are strong enough from months of using the chair, the various walkers, crutches, etc. to propel me forward. I can move my left leg while keeping the right out of its path. I am swimming. I do only 2 laps in my small pool, but it might as well have been Olympic size for how tired I am. I may never dive in, but dammit I will swim. He did not take that from me.

BOUNDARIES

The cane is my Siamese twin - we are never apart. While my hip and leg seemingly work, they do not do so well. Nor do my legs know how to play nice with each other. I don't want to take a chance that anything I do could jeopardize what I feel is my last chance. I understand my boundaries.

The surgeon said while in the house when I felt stronger I could try little steps without the cane. I can hold onto the counter or the table or a chair. I start to do so. I lean the cane against the counter in the kitchen as I do minimal tasks like making a sandwich or making coffee.

As I test my walking I am reminded of an old children's toy, Weebles - they wobble but they don't fall down. That's what I look like. My gait is so off you might think I was having a seizure. Nope, just taking a stroll around the kitchen. It's how I roll now.

Hope this gets better.

YESTERDAY TODAY AND TOMORROW

It was yesterday. It was a lifetime ago. It is today. Today is my 2nd Crashaversary. I feel different from last year, but with so many elements of my life that are hauntingly familiar.

I keep writing this journal for me. Sometimes I spend time and go back and make changes so the writing flows better. Sometimes I just leave it as is - the jumble of the words mirrors my thoughts and feelings. Today I will make no changes. And that's ok.

This time last year I was planning for a surgery. I had no idea one would become two. That the roller coaster of quick progress from the first would plummet into horrific pain and being back in that chair. I went from tremendous hope to being broken again.

The last 365 days has not been easy. I started over from scratch but this time without as many expectations. I couldn't tell everyone that what had happened - the multiple surgeries had left me with no belief of a positive outcome. Of how there were nights I would listen to make sure everyone was asleep upstairs before I cried in my pillow in the guest room downstairs separated from my family. They only know of a few "bad days".

Had I been without a support system of family and friends I would have given up. But I am blessed with people near and far, and even new people put in my path that added prayers and distractions. I tried my best to keep up the brave and happy facade as I did not want others to break as I was broken. I needed to draw in their strength to buoy mine. All my relationships became symbiotic. Which is ok.

Without any second thought those close rallied around me. "Babysitting" so I did not have to go back into a rehab center as I could not be on my own and allowing John to work and giving him a few moments of peace. Sitting watching mindless TV shows and sharing simple meals, just making time go lightly. Time turned out to be on my side as shortly after I was liberated from the chair, the world went on lockdown. I am not sure I could have made it through that time without the human contact.

Since then, I continue to make increments of small progress. Baby steps if you will. This upcoming crashaversary though had me understandably focusing on the negatives. Changes we will make to the house now that we know what my limits are. A different car that will be easier to get in and out of, rather than the SUV that has provided me comfort. The fact that while it is physically taxing to try the stairs, the mental struggle leaves me needing a nap after. I have only tackled the stairs about a dozen times. My muscles contract with just the thought. The continued doctor visits. The Boom was 2 years ago, but I am still within a year of the last surgery. My health issues reflect the damage of the Boom still. Even today as I showered the Boom continues to mock me. I may never be able to rid myself of the shower chair. I experience difficulty getting dressed as my right side will still not cooperate 100%. I have a few pairs of jeans that are made with stretch material to allow for decrease pressure and the inevitable swelling on the

Boom side. I decided to try on my "normal" jeans as these are showing wear. Nope. The pressure on the Boom side from just a simple pair of pants hurt. Even now, even 2 years from the Boom. I learned that 50% of one of the muscles was removed, a fact I missed along the way. I threw my old life away and new jeans are on the way. I still can't tie my sneakers and still need the kids elastic self-closures. I am haunted by the words of one of the therapists- each day you have to learn to live like this. That is what I am dealing with now - that has been my pity party these last few weeks. This is pretty much as good as it may get. I have to learn to live like this.

But - oh the positives! My husband and children are healthy in this pandemic age. I can make my own coffee without John having to leave everything on the counter. I can get my own cereal and milk. I can even make an egg as I can stand and lean long enough at the stove. I do my own laundry. On most days I can load the dishwasher. I can safely shower by myself if no one is home. I can get on the patio alone - no more wheeling up to the open slider and being stuck inside the house. I can drive a up to a little more than 1/2 an hour. I can use the pool, albeit I need the cane to get in and out safely. I can get dressed without having to use the dressing stick. I can watch tv on the couch. I still use the chair as it provides comfort when I sit, but that is by choice not necessity. But that's ok.

Last year I Face Timed with my LLBFF, and we had a virtual donut party. F' He Who Will Not Be Named. We bet he wasn't having donuts with his friends.

LLBFF wanted to connect today. We both had potential commitments that would make the timing a bit off. It would take nothing to make it work. With the pandemic donut procurement is low on the list. A package arrived yesterday of cookies shaped like donuts. She ordered the same for her house. I will check in later. Right now, at this moment I am not ready. But that's ok.

I went in the pool. I haven't been in for a few weeks and made up for it on this beautiful sunny day. I did my leg exercises, swam a bit, listened to music and just relaxed. I took time today to be normal. No stress, no talk of the BOOM, no reminders of the last 2 years. I spent hours outside, just me. I showered, I napped. I had a plain old lazy Saturday. I had an ok day. That's what I needed today - I needed to be ok if only for a few hours. I needed to feel things are ok. I needed not to let what I feel for that man and what he did to me, and by extension those close to me, not to be the focus of this day. Today he has no bearing on me, I'm ok.

I will have my cookie later. I will most likely say F' him tomorrow. But you know what? That's ok.

WARDROBE ENHANCEMENT

I will be going to see the surgeon in a few months. He has been on my mind, maybe more than he should be. We have an odd relationship. I know my case was difficult. Yet he ALWAYS spoke with such conviction. Not due to arrogance, but in his heart, he believed, and he hoped with me. He became invested because he promised me, I would walk. I have never had a doctor promise anything, not even something small. We have spoken about our families, our work, and of course meg-leg. I believe in my heart that no one else could have done better, it was just the seriousness of my injuries.

I wonder if he will be as apprehensive about our next meeting as I am.

On a previous visit I wore my handicap parking shirt. He enjoyed that and it broke some of the tension. I purchased a new shirt that has the Periodic element for Titanium, and states AFTER MARKET PARTS. I will wear this for my next visit.

DEPOSITION TIME

This will be the only mention of my legal woes. I write this so others will know what to expect.

The courts are starting to open again, virtually, in this COVID world. The deposition we have been fighting to do virtually for the last year (as I can't travel) is now REQUIRED to be virtual. This is my life. My lawyer spends some time walking me through the process. We talk about my life. It's harder discussing it with a virtual stranger. It's been a while, but I cry over my losses.

The day of the deposition comes. He Who Will Not be Named is not online - that is his choice. There are a number of people in attendance. Strangers who get to question every aspect of my life.

My lawyer advised me to pause between questions - before I answer in case he has to object from over 1,000 miles away. I do so without needing to think about it - every question is like pouring alcohol in a wound.

Funny thing, well maybe that's not the best phrase to use, is the least number of questions has to do with the actual BOOM. Guess they understood you couldn't provide a great amount of details for the time you were unconscious. Yet for the moments I was awake - well let's just say I can remember the details that haunt me still. They ask nothing of the rehab hell - smart move on their part. If this goes to trial, I will make sure they all have to hear every miserable detail.

They ask numbers. I have been keeping detailed records that I supply to my lawyer. They subpoenaed records from the last decade of things that had nothing to do with the BOOM. I reply I didn't know I was to bring the data that they have been supplied multiple times. They press. I stand my ground. I tell them I know the have the info, if not get it from my attorney. I've incurred many more multipliers of expenses and medical charges than he has insurance for. Give me a break. Pain and suffering doesn't even look like it's a factor as we fight to cover my bills, and then the lienholders swoop in. In a BOOM everyone wants their share back.

The lawyer then concentrates on my life NOW post BOOM. Wants to know any changes. I know he is looking for something big. I start to state the facts - emotions aside. I list all the things I can't do. I spew my limitations. But he presses on.

That's when I notice he is wearing a wedding ring. I pause. I say I know you are looking for big things. I mention his ring. I ask if he ever calls his wife to pick up milk on the way home. He does not answer. I tell him my husband can't. For me to pick up a gallon of milk will take at least 45 minutes. I will have to hope there is a handicapped parking spot. I explain how difficult it is to push a cart. I explain my knowledge of how much a gallon of milk weighs. I tell him how taxing it is to get back and forth and in and out of my car.

I admit to not cooking. But I used to be on cleanup duty. Doing dishes, pots, pans etc. I can't do that anymore. Another task that falls to someone else to pick up.

I speak of clearing the table. Nope, can't do that either, unless I want to make one trip per plate or glass.

I let him know of my progress with the dishwasher. Then I explain I can't put most things away. Same issue as clearing. I either need to do things one at a time or can't reach or bend steadily enough to put things away.

I tell him it's not the big things, but the 100 little things daily that changed our lives forever. He doesn't ask me anything else.

The house phone keeps ringing. The telemarketers are in overdrive since the lockdown - they know someone is home. After like the 4th attempt, I excuse myself to turn off the ringer.

When I come back, a woman who has said nothing so far except introducing herself pauses and asks me if that is a wheelchair I am in.

I too pause, and state yes. Sitting for long periods of time hurts my ass tablet. I also need chair arms to lift myself up. I tried to use other chairs but find it difficult to move away from the table. The wheelchair works best. Not what I want, but what I understand makes my life more manageable.

She says nothing.

I tell her she did not notice the steps I need to get out of the chair as the camera is facing higher. I move the camera down. I then walk her through the steps I go through hundreds of times. As I am talking, I explain I am unlocking the wheels, moving the chair back from the table, re-engaging the locks, making sure the strap for my cane is around my wrist, I use both hands on the arms and lift myself, I move the cane and off I go. Then reverse the process when I sit.

Silence.

I tell her I can do it quickly as I do this all day every day. I tell her this is my life.

They are done.

I am done.

I am devastated. I am broken. I hate that they were able to delve into my life. A friend comforts me - but I have a heart filled with anger.

THIS IS WHAT SUCCESS LOOKS LIKE

Today is one year from what I hoped was my last surgery. One year from when I thought there would be no piecing me back together – that finally I was so broken literally and figuratively I could never be fixed. One year since I again had someone holding my hand in a hospital so I was not alone as I faced the prospect of hoping that I would be ok.

This has been a horrific year on a global scale. Each month the world prays that the upcoming one will be better – and it's not. So today is Friday the 13th. If ever this year were to have a cursed day, I would believe it to be today. Yet here I was meeting with my surgeon to determine the level of success of this last surgery – to see if the bone had not only lived but thrived. To see if the prosthesis remained in place. To see, to hope, that my journey was coming to an end on a positive note. I would be less than truthful if I stated I expected a positive result. I made the decision to go by myself. I cannot face John or the kids if the news is bad. I don't know what I will do. My expectations are on the morose side.

The surgeon passes by as I sit while I wait for x-rays – he looks at the cane and only says hi. In I go, x-rays done, and I am waiting for the doctor. The assistant loads the pictures on the pc and leaves. I can't wait. I get up and start to go through the files myself – by now I know what I am looking for. Overall, they look good – but I notice some areas that don't show growth. I continue to go through my on-line files.

He comes in and I skip niceties – "what is with the black area?" He replies loudly –

"it's all good! You are all good! – you are fine!!!"

"But what about the black areas?" I only need 30% good growth in the right place – we both look at the screen and exclaim I have so much more than that!!!

The bone has grown around the broken screws (which could not safely be removed) – the prosthetic is solidly in place. The places where the bone did not grow is ok. It's not dead, it just can't grow. He looks at me and we laugh as we say together "because I was in a serious accident." He says he was worried when he saw me sitting there with the cane. He didn't know what to say and wanted to wait until he saw the pictures.

Now we talk about discomfort, stairs, driving, sleeping on my stomach – everything and anything to do with the BOOM. The good news is that even though part of the muscle is gone, and I have been sliced and diced 1,000 ways to Sunday – the fact that there was recent progress means there is more to come. More work – more improvement. I have another year to heal – to progress – to live my life. He gives me instructions on what to do next, exercises to help continuing to retrain my broken ass tablet. How to listen to my body. I can deal with everything now. Piece of cake. Fucking Ironman.

I will most likely always have a limp, but hopefully not as pronounced. I will also most likely always need the cane to some extent. Stairs are down the road but in my future. I have no restrictions as of today for the first time in a long time. I will see him in a year. Covid took away our ability to hug – both he and I probably would have if no one else was in the room. He loved the shirt and took a picture to show his wife.

So today I embark on the journey to my next step. It has been 786 days since the BOOM – but it the last day I will count. Today I look only forward not back.

For those who have been on this long journey to my first step – I don't know how to articulate what is in my heart. The fact that I am so lost for words today to express how I feel about all of you should speak mountains. I am only where I am because of you – family, friends, doctors, nurses, strangers. You all played a monumental part in my healing – body and soul. Your faith when mine was wavering, your assistance when my body was broken, your gifts when I felt alone, your time that could have been given elsewhere. Your words and encouragement when I thought I could handle no more. Your hand when I needed comfort. I could go on and on.

Thank you. Simple but sincere.

Love you all –

EPILOGUE

I stopped counting days awhile back. All of us crash survivors understand counting days - days to get up, days to use the bathroom alone, days to walk that first step. But I fell back to counting today, 1266 – the number of days since I last have slept in my own bed.

The BOOM took away my mobility for a long time, and even though outwardly I have been looking "fine" we all know I was not, or still am not. We don't often talk about what goes on within our walls. The need for a wheelchair sometimes still. I use it daily as well to sit at the table, it brings a relief to my injury site that I have not been able to replicate with any other chair. The adaptive tools that have become part of our lives is now, in my case, going to be with me indefinitely. Orthotics and lifts in my sneakers to make my legs the same size. The bed rails…well you can see; the list goes on and on.

I am lucky enough that we have a guest bedroom downstairs. It has been my room since I returned from rehab. I never fully moved in because doing so would admit defeat. I have the things I tried to direct my family to bring downstairs for me in addition to new things I bought over the last years. This was "just for a short while" so I was not moving permanently. 1266 days after the BOOM and I am still there, until tonight.

The doctor told me stairs will be my last challenge. While I physically I am getting stronger, I have panic attacks coming down. He explained that I have been put back together differently. My gait and center now make me feel as I am lurching forward, and down. I have to learn how to compensate. I am missing muscle – literally as it was damaged and removed. My bones and screws and prosthetics and other pieces do not match my non-operative side. How could it? My legs are no longer the same length. I will know when it is time.

It is time.

I have been practicing the stairs – and was taken aback by what my 2nd floor had become. Let's just say my family was surprised to see me upstairs and realized some "organization" was needed.

Today I went upstairs to start to reclaim one of the last pieces of my life. I went through draw after draw that I have not opened in 3 years. I went through my closet. I purged bag after bag of things that did not survive the neglect or were no longer of any good to me. It was a visit to whom I used to be. Then I started to go through things I had forgotten about but still hold meaning for me. Awards the kids received through the years, handmade "Mom coupons" I have saved (good for a hug or a kiss), pictures, a rock my sister gave me.

I felt angry for a good while – what that driver took away from me that I forgot. I was mad at myself for forgetting. I should not have needed these tangible things to keep these memories. I was mad at myself for getting mad rather than focusing on what I was reclaiming.

I needed to refocus – or I could continue to spiral. It's easy to get lost in yourself. I moved forward and continued to reminisce through this sensory journey of my own things. In the end I was happier for it.

I write this today because we are all on a journey, whether at the beginning or well on the way. There will be days like today – I hope you too can work through it. I am exhausted as I took the stairs several times. I am sore – my BOOM side feels every step I take. But I will be sleeping in MY bed, with thoughts of those who helped me get there.

ABOUT THE AUTHOR

Journey to my First Step is Candi Puleo's debut book. Originally from New York, she and her family have called South Florida home for over 27 years.

The "BOOM" inspired her to take readers on her honest journey of recovery – both physical and emotional when she couldn't find the answers she was seeking. "What can I expect? What's next? How do I learn - to live like this?"

www.ingramcontent.com/pod-product-compliance
Lightning Source LLC
La Vergne TN
LVHW051408080426
835508LV00022B/2992